TO HUNT IN THE MORNING

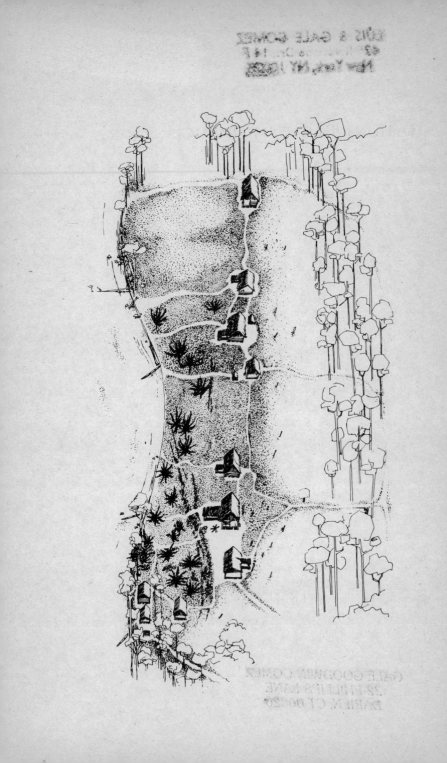

JANET SISKIND

To
Hunt
in the
Morning

OXFORD UNIVERSITY PRESS
London   Oxford   New York

OXFORD UNIVERSITY PRESS

Oxford London Glasgow

New York Toronto Melbourne Wellington

Ibadan Nairobi Dar es Salaam Cape Town

Kuala Lumpur Singapore Jakarta Hong Kong Tokyo

Delhi Bombay Calcutta Madras Karachi

This reprint, 1978

Copyright © 1973 Oxford University Press, Inc.
Library of Congress Catalogue Card Number 73-82674
First published by Oxford University Press, New York, 1973
First issued as an Oxford University Press paperback, 1975
Printed in the United States of America

To Ndaishiwaka, Yawandi, Bashkondi, Samuel

ACKNOWLEDGMENTS

Fieldwork among the Sharanahua was funded by the Comisión Fulbright del Peru, the Instituto de Psiquiatria Social of the Universidad de San Marcos, with the assistance of Foundations Fund for Research in Psychiatry, The American Philosophical Society, and the Research Council of Rutgers University. An Ogden Mills Fellowship from the American Museum of Natural History provided the time and facilities for the analysis of field data.

I wish to thank Alexander Alland, Jr., for his suggestions and comments on the manuscript and Marc Rice for the maps and rendering of the village of Marcos. I am grateful to my students whose interest in the Sharanahua has been an encouragement and a guide in writing this book.

Many people have influenced my work through their writing or conversation. Here I will mention only a few of the most immediate and general sources which shape this book: A view of ecological adaptation as a primary relationship, Robert Carneiro and Andrew Peter Vayda; a search for structure in the analysis of ethnography, myth, social organization, and shamanism, Claude Lévi-Strauss and Robert Murphy; psychological assumptions and interpretations are based on Harry Stack Sullivan, Jane Pearce, and Saul Newton; an approach to the beauty and the limits of primitive society, Karl Marx. Where sources have been used for a particular topic they are given in the chapter notes. The experiences, the faults, and the interpretations are mine.

CONTENTS

"Hence in one way the childlike world of the ancients appears to be superior; and this is so, in so far as we seek for closed shape, form and established limitation. The ancients provide a narrow satisfaction, whereas the modern world leaves us unsatisfied, or, where it appears to be satisfied with itself, is *vulgar* and *mean.*"

—Karl Marx, *Pre-Capitalist Economic Formations*

TO HUNT IN THE MORNING

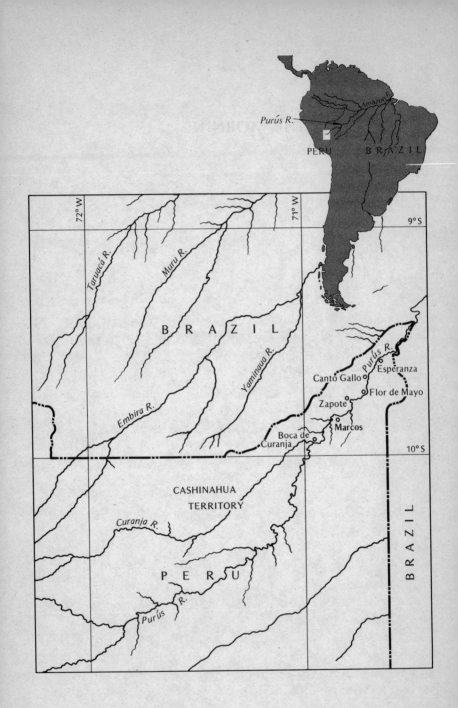

1

INTRODUCTION

The Anthropologist and the People

The day I left Marcos for the last time, Samuel and Gustavo paddled the canoe; Naikashu, Yawandi, and Ishamba, Gustavo's young wife and their smaller children came along. Baiyakondi was sick, and his son, Ndaishiwaka, who had planned to travel with us, stayed behind to chant the curing songs in Baiyakondi's *mosquitero*. We piled the skins, my equipment, our rolled-up hammocks and *mosquiteros* with the poles tied up, a pot full of cold manioc, a bunch of bananas, a basketful of raw manioc still in its hard brown husk, and two machetes on long sticks placed lengthwise in the canoe to protect everything from the water that would soon leak or rain into the bottom of the canoe.

At nine o'clock that morning it was still cool, the August sky bright blue with high white clouds. We crowded onto the narrow seats of the dugout, Samuel paddling easily in back, Gustavo in front with his metal-tipped harpoon ready at hand. As we paddled across to cut to the inner curve, Gustavo searched the water, rising to his feet with his harpoon poised. Samuel stopped paddling, the canoe drifted, no one spoke. The harpoon flashed into the water and bobbed up again empty. Gustavo hauled it back and rewound the rope attaching the point to the shaft. Several times we waited while Gustavo threw the harpoon, gesturing to Samuel to shift direction. By twelve o'clock he had pulled in three large fish, and the sun had become a terrible hammer. We scooped up the coolness of the river and drenched our hats and hair and within minutes were again dried out and burning. An hour later we had paddled into storm clouds and tried to get to the beach where some traveler, stopping for the night, had once built a crude shelter, a few Y-shaped upright poles stuck into the sand with a horizontal pole resting in the crotches, a couple of large fronds of palm thatch across the top providing insufficient protection from the rain which began to pour down. Although we shivered with cold and the discomfort of wet sand, we tried to protect our equipment rather than ourselves since if the hammocks and *mosquiteros* were soaked it would be a cold, miserable, sleepless night. Despite the rain, Naikashu had a fire going and the fish cooking within ten minutes, and an hour later the rain let up and we ate huge, delicious portions of fish and steamed manioc.

Gustavo and Samuel shoveled the water out of the canoe with their paddles and dried it with handfuls of leaves. The cargo was repacked and protected with large thatch fronds on top, and the trip continued. Heading toward a small beach, a slight motion of leaves, a whispered, "Jaguar!" and Samuel rapidly guided the canoe over, but no one had brought a shotgun. As we got close Gustavo leaped into the water, grasping the harpoon and rushed into the trees behind the sand. A paca ran out and stood frozen on the beach so that Gustavo was able to spear it with the harpoon and then smash it on the head with his machete. He ran back into the trees after another one, and two fat pacas were added to the canoe load.

About two o'clock in the afternoon it started to rain again, lightly but continuously so that everyone was cold, wet, and miserable. The small children huddled in the women's laps for warmth and fell asleep. No one said a word as if to conserve energy for warmth and survival. Three endless, chilled hours and again the rain stopped as we pulled the canoe up on the beach near Canto Gallo. There was a small shelter there, and the men rapidly added three more sections, enough for the four large *mosquiteros*.

Naikashu started her fire, everyone bathed and changed into the clothes that had been so carefully protected from the rain. Yawandi and Ishamba cleaned and skinned the two pacas and stowed the pieces away in a basket for the next day. We finished what remained of the fish and drank sweet, hot banana drink and got into our hammocks with a plate of hot coals underneath warming the entire *mosquitero,* warm, dry, and well fed.

I first came to the Upper Purús in late August of 1966, planning to spend the night at Marcos and to travel further upriver the following day to another Sharanahua village called Boca de Curanja. The American missionaries at Marcos were extremely generous and suggested that as they were leaving the village in ten days I might prefer to stay there and offered the use of their house. The beginning of fieldwork is a terrifying period, when the problems of where to sleep, eat, and survive are overwhelming, and I eagerly accepted. As it turned out, working at Marcos rather than Boca de Curanja was a good choice, though living in the missionaries' house, somewhat removed from the village, was a mistake. (I later moved to a house more centrally located, which luckily had been left empty.)

Despite my conviction that no one would be interested in talking to a stranger, I began to meet the people of Marcos by treating the sick. I was soon inundated with visitors. The missionaries had forbidden Sharanahua to enter their small house but encouraged them to congregate on the screened porch where a two-way radio was kept for communication with the mission base. Everyone at Marcos seemed to spend part of his day, starting early in the morning, watching what I was doing through the screened window between the porch and kitchen. I found the constant audience unnerving.

At times I left my own house and anxiously wandered through the rest of the village, meeting continual questions as to what I was doing. A few people invited me into their houses, and I would sit for a few minutes, trying to endure the strain of listening to an incomprehensible language and the continuous attack of gnats. I could not understand their names or distinguish faces for more than a moment, though I remember Bashkondi, sitting up on the raised floor at the entrance to her house, hacking the tough shell of a palm nut with a machete, smiling and offering me a taste. I would return to my house to meet the onslaught of five to ten people asking me for things and commenting on what I did.

The difficulty of endlessly dealing with this number of people led me to notice that the Sharanahua did not behave in this way with anyone else in the village. At no other house did people appear, stay, and stare. People could be seen to visit: a lone man, two or three women. People occasionally begged each other for things, but only a few people, and if ignored they left. I started to realize that despite the open houses there were unseen barriers that prevented free entry between Sharanahua. I began to ally myself with a few households while ignoring the demands and visits of others. In part the choice of households was forced upon me by Zacharais, a Sharanahua of about sixty years of age, an important man at Marcos. The day I arrived he gave me the name of his older sister, Fando, and stopped by my house early each morning, saying, "Are you awake, older sister? Give me a cigarette." Since an older sister is expected to be generous, Zacharais always accented the relationship despite my protests that he was far older than I. I began to acknowledge this relationship, freely meeting Zacharais' demands and those of the other members of his household.

Two of Zacharais' daughters lived close by, both married to Basta, and they too were willing to validate the fiction of kinship between us. Basta is sometimes referred to by a word that can be translated as "chief" or "headman." However, he has no real authority nor does he direct or attempt to organize any activities outside of his own household. When fights break out in the village between drunken men, Basta along with the other older men and women tries to cool tempers and talks or threatens sense into the combatants. Basta's house is most often the site of dancing or the place where Peruvians stop when they travel the river, and it was the household that first offered me its hospitality and begged me for kerosene.

Samuel, Zacharais' son, moved his house and family three times during the three years I knew him. When I arrived at Marcos he and his wife and their three daughters had just moved into a new house which Samuel had started to build when his first son-in-law moved in. A few months later the son-in-law left, and Samuel returned to his father's house. The new house stood empty, and Samuel gladly accepted a box of shotgun shells and the promise of my coffee pot to let me live in it.

I maintained the fiction of kinship with the related households of Zacharais, Basta, and Samuel, visiting them almost every day while seldom entering other houses. I gave them gifts of kerosene, cloth, and soap and evaded the requests of others. I learned the Sharanahua art of lying. I would say sorrowfully, "I have no more soap," and someone would say, "You're lying." I would deny it mildly since it is not insulting to be called a liar at Marcos. A direct refusal is experienced as an insult which implies that someone has no right to ask you, but a lie, even when discovered, as inevitably it is, may be shrugged off with a smile. While I continued to give medicine to everyone at Marcos, I kept otherwise distant from all but one other household.

This was the household of Ndaishiwaka, a man forty years of age, who has two wives and eight children. Ndaishiwaka is one of the three shamans at Marcos, and, like them, he takes part in the everyday world of hunting, fishing, and agriculture, but also enters the world of the spirits. He is a subtle man, sensitive to mood, and never entered my house except when I

Ndaishiwaka

wished for company. When, after two months, I ran out of kerosene for my stove he helped me find wood for my fire, called my son and myself to eat in his household, spent evenings drinking coffee, smoking my cigarettes, and talking.

One cannot buy food at Marcos, and gaining access to meat, fish, and vegetables was a continual problem. I had brought some supplies to Marcos, but eating tuna fish from a can while the smell of deer meat cooking spreads from the next house is painful, and my supplies were insufficient. At first, I followed the missionary's example of giving things away evenhandedly, giving every man a shotgun shell in the hope of receiving meat, accepting eggs from every woman and searching for a return gift. Keeping track of this was impossible and further embroiled me in the hopeless task of dealing equally with every individual at Marcos.

I wanted to be able to eat with the Sharanahua to increase my knowledge and rapport, to enjoy their good food, and to avoid the constant chore of cooking and cleaning up. I finally learned to make a generous gift of a box of shells to the four households I spent time with, asking them to call me when they had a lot of meat. Basta's and Ndaishiwaka's households often sent a child to say, "Fando, come, let's eat." I also learned the Sharanahua's style of appearing in a house, saying that one has come to talk, while waiting to see if food will be served. I reciprocated to these households usually by serving coffee, crackers, and jam at my house in the evenings. Occasionally I cooked spaghetti and invited a few of the members of a household to eat.

At times when I found life at Marcos frustrating and bitterly lonely, I revenged myself childishly by eating crackers and jam alone in my *mosquitero,* opening the large can as quietly as possible since children can hear a cracker can opening over an incredible distance. Despite my caution someone would come by and ask what I was doing. I would reply that I was reading, though no one believed me. Giving and receiving food are important emotion-laden interactions at Marcos. Eating with people is an affirmation of kinship. Refusing to share food is a denial of all relationship, a statement that the other is an outsider. When people are eating and offer nothing one feels more than hunger, one feels alien and alienated.

My solutions to the apparently simple problems of getting enough to eat at Marcos began a process of involvement that led beyond my initial ideas of what I planned to learn from the Sharanahua. I can distinguish three stages in my experiences with the Sharanahua and in my development as an anthropologist. The first stage is a view of the Sharanahua as objects of study, a primitive culture with a history and a location, tropical forest Indians of eastern Peru. In this view they are the laboratory of the comparative social scientist, whose differences from ourselves drive a wedge into our ethnocentrism, providing a wider view of what to include under the rubric of "human nature." They exist, they are there, they are different, so that one cannot say that to be human is to be monogamous, ambitious, avaricious; human values need not include an ethic of absolute honesty or compassion; it is good to lie, steal, kill, under certain circumstances.

The project that took me to the field dealt with the problem of how a primitive people interact and adapt to the particular diseases in their environment, whether taboos on food or post-natal behavior, for example, have a rational base regardless of the people's knowledge or lack of knowledge about germ theory. The nature of the problem led me to look for a relatively unacculturated people, whose way of life was still indigenous rather than Peruvian, who were not in a position to make use of modern medicine.

The Sharanahua had been pacified for twenty-five years; they wore Peruvian clothing, but they somewhat fit these speci-fications. Their subsistence methods were their own, they spent very little time working for a *patrón,* a Peruvian trader; and no missionary had yet succeeded in converting them to a belief in God or in convincing them of the Christian ethic.

I found out quickly at Marcos that even though most of the men spoke some Spanish, it was extremely limited. If I asked questions in Spanish, they were reluctant to admit they could not understand and tended to answer any way they were able. I had no confidence in such answers. Despite my difficulties in learning to speak Sharanahua, I found it the only reliable mode of communication, though for months it was frustrating to be unable to ask what I wanted to know or to understand the answers.

In the early months of fieldwork it was of some comfort to collect a steadily increasing fund of data on the medical symp-toms produced by eighty-nine people. However, no patterns emerged and no relationship between sickness and taboos was evidenced. It appeared unlikely that I would be able to write a thesis on this subject. In contrast, hunting, which was obviously a major focus of Sharanahua life, seemed to be a topic that would lead both to an understanding of their society and an acceptable dissertation.

The self-seeking motive of obtaining a degree, the key to my profession, a rational motive in my society, led me to view the Sharanahua at times as those wonderful people who would help me to obtain my degree and to see myself as yet another foreign exploiter; at times to view them as an incredible nuisance who continually sidestepped or blocked my fieldwork and to see myself as varying from a hard-working success to a lazy failure. The real world for me lay in the department of anthropology of my university and among my friends in New York. The ethics of my background as well as those of anthropology led me to try to be as unexploiting as possible—fair, for example, in giving gifts for services. The methods of ethnographic research, participant observation and work with informants, led me into an increasing involvement with several people at Marcos. With the exception of a few specific bodies of data, most of my information was derived from participant observation. My main companions were the women and children of Basta's, Samuel's, and Ndaishiwaka's households, my particular friends, Bashkondi and Yawandi. On my first stay in Marcos of approximately six months, with a long break after the first four, my son, then nine years old, traveled with me, and, to a certain extent, made it easier for women to deal with me. True, in their eyes, I was partly incomprehensible, a woman traveling far from her own kin group, but the fact that like most women I had a child was an immediate point of rapport. It also provided me with information on children that would otherwise have been unattainable or simply unnoticed.

I learned the language in the long, hot afternoons, sitting with Bashkondi, learning to pick seeds out of cotton, watching her older half-sister and co-wife, Naikashu, mend her daughter's dress. Bashkondi would call as I walked hesitantly by the house, "Fando, come in," and made room in the wide hammock, shifting to one side so I could lounge at the other end, facing her diagonally. Hammocks are slung low at Marcos, and Bashkondi kept the hammock moving with one foot pushing against the floor. Naikashu, a practical and efficient woman, was impersonally pleasant to me. As I grew to know the household better she often included me in the command, "Let's eat," and made demands for kerosene, cloth for her children's dresses, needles and thread. A woman in her forties, she seldom paints her face and wears ragged, worn-out dresses, saving the best materials for her sixteen-year-old and six-year-old daughters. Competent, incurious, hard working, she directed the women of this large household.

Bashkondi, about twenty-eight years old, is a beautiful woman. Frequently in the afternoon she would carefully paint her face and put on all her beads. She said that she did not like her husband and had only one lover and that he spent more time with other women. She repeatedly asked questions about my travels, my kin, my country and the men who lived there. She said she wanted to see my country, but that she would die in the cold. She teased her two sons, caressed them, ignored them, and wept when her eight year old went with his kinsmen on a two-day fishing trip. She begged seductively for beads and better cloth than the traders sell—bright solid red that I brought from Pucallpa. Bashkondi often painted my face, laughing at its shape which made the flat designs seem awkward. She found my hair incomprehensible, combing it to make it lie down and saying, "Why is your hair so big?" and then noticed that when wet it was thinner than her own strong, black hair. At times she pretended admiration for my reddish frizzy hair, but laughed and agreed when I called her a liar.

Yawandi, Basta's oldest daughter, painted herself less often and gave the cloth and beads she received from me to her fifteen-year-old daughter. Yawandi is a strong and independent woman of about thirty-two whose mother died long ago. She has been married twice, her first husband is dead and she left her second when he drunkenly beat her while she was pregnant. Yawandi said that she preferred not to marry again, though for years she has been Samuel's mistress, and he is the father of her six-year-old son. She had washed clothes for the missionaries and she asked to wash mine, saying she had no husband to give her trade goods. She spoke a few words of Spanish, which is rare for a woman at Marcos, and was able to construct sentences in Sharanahua that I could understand long before I could comprehend most conversations. She knew a good deal of herbal medicines, was an expert midwife, and enjoyed relating myths and gossip. Perhaps our similar odd status for Marcos as single women drew us together. All the women at Marcos and many of the men were shorter than I am, but it always startled me to notice that Yawandi was not my height. I remember returning from a long trip through the forest, stumbling with fatigue as we reached Basta's house, and Yawandi's holding out to me, as to a sister, a bowl of sweet hot banana drink.

Bashkondi, Yawandi, and I often bathed together late in the afternoon, partly for sociability, partly to share my soap, with Samuel's three young daughters tagging along. The women said they admired my lighter skin. They found body hair repulsive though they were polite, and they laughed when I asked if it hurt to pull out the pubic hair they meticulously removed. Even when women bathe together they are discreetly modest, removing their skirts above their heads as they enter the river, crouching to completely conceal their genitals when they emerge. I imitated them, though with far less grace.

An anthropologist in the field is pulled in two opposing directions: to maintain a role in the society under study and to obtain data that goes beyond a participant's knowledge of his own society. To the extent that I wished to participate in the everyday activities of Marcos as a familiar equal, I had to accept the limits that Sharanahua culture places on women. Occasionally, especially in the first few months at Marcos, I

Yawandi and Bashkondi

would be invited on a fishing trip and eagerly prepare to go. Many fishing trips include both men and women, but at times an all male trip occurred. Before I reached the canoe one of the women would stop me and tell me not to go, saying that we are not going, you will be raped. I did not believe the threat, but I realized that ignoring it would remove me from a role in which women were at ease with me and shared information and gossip as with an equal. A male anthropologist, of course, would have the same limitation, prohibiting easy conversations with women. (It is a common folk belief of our own culture that this is not a serious problem.)

My work with male informants did not fit into any role in Sharanahua society and was, for that reason, often difficult and tense. Since the men at Marcos had had some experience with missionaries who worked with a linguistic informant, Samuel and other men who wished to work with me placed the interaction in this framework. My curiosity about nonlinguistic matters was considered frivolous. Basta often reprimanded me for spending so much time with the foolish women of his household, telling me I would be better off if I stayed in my house and studied as the missionary did. I denied the missionary role since it would seriously restrict the kinds of information that people shared with me. Everyone at Marcos liked and respected the missionary couple and did their best not to disturb them with gossip that might be upsetting, and gossip is invaluable to an anthropologist. My verbal statements of differences between myself and the missionaries were far less convincing than the fact that I smoked heavily and, more important, that when Ndaishiwaka offered me a drink from a bottle of cane liquor I accepted with honest and evident pleasure.

My first informant was Samuel, who spoke some Spanish and, as I slowly learned, had a particularly difficult accent in his own language. In general I found that young men spoke more clearly than old, but Samuel, who was in his thirties, was always hard to follow. He spoke with extreme rapidity and impatiently demanded what else he should tell me. He wanted to be my informant, but I found it unproductive and annoying to work with him. When I changed informants our relationship was strained and awkward, and not until I returned to Marcos a year later, the summer of 1968, was it possible to renew a relatively easy-going friendship. At that point Samuel had again moved his house, and taken a son-in-law, and I lived in the son-in-law's house next to Samuel and his wife, Ifama. Their daughters often slept in my house, I regularly ate with the household, and occasionally spent evenings talking to Samuel and Ifama.

Samuel is attracted to and afraid of Peruvian culture. He plays at acting like a Peruvian, builds houses that are too large, hunts poorly, and is stingy with his rare good catch of

Samuel

fish. He seems pulled between Peruvian culture and his own, and rarely succeeds at either. In contrast Ndaishiwaka plays his own culture well—a good hunter, generous to his kinsmen —and he encourages his second wife's affair with a trader to ensure trade goods. Ndaishiwaka has taken the cultural solution of those who feel unduly confined by Sharanahua culture. In becoming a shaman he has made use of his desire to go beyond his social world in a way provided for and respected by Sharanahua society.

Ndaishiwaka was my second informant, and we worked mainly on shaman's songs, curing techniques, case histories, and his own life history. Like other men who had learned some Spanish numbers he sprinkled his history with them, and I would dutifully write them down until I realized that he had no real understanding of how Spanish numbers work nor a numerical idea of how many years ago something actually occurred. Sharanahua numbers go from one to five, after that they jump to "two hands," then many, "two hands and two feet." There are past years and future years but no fixed point from which to count. The dates that I used in tracing his history and others' are based on estimates of people's ages. Ndaishiwaka would say, "When I first met Chatafundia, before she became my wife, she was Tarani's size," and I can estimate that Tarani is approximately fourteen since she seems close to puberty but has not yet begun to menstruate. Through cross checking several life histories it is possible to approximate when a village was moved or when someone was born. I assume I am accurate within a five-year range. Ndaishiwaka like Yawandi was extraordinarily sensitive to the level at which I could understand the language.

Yawandi worked with me as an informant the last time I was at Marcos, the summer of 1969. She had always been a valuable source of information and, in addition, she was incredibly patient at the slow job of transcribing myths from tape to writing. We would listen to the previous night's tape of Basta or Baiyakondi telling a myth. She would first summarize it briefly and then recite line by line as I played the tape so that I could write them down. We would then go back over every sentence as I struggled for a word-by-word understanding. Yawandi had difficulty with the concept of fixing meaning within a particular word or phrase, preferring to explain the story, but she sat through the hours of work, sharing my hammock as I wrote at one end, and adding gossip to the slow work.

The first six months of fieldwork during 1966–67 were at times exciting, often depressing, a mixture of loneliness and satisfaction, exotic wonder and stifling boredom. I left Marcos in May, with relief, to return to English, friends, and the dissertation. Yet, my work felt unfinished, and as I waited for the verdict on my thesis I wrote a research proposal to return the following summer. The words of Basta's son, said reproachfully when I left, stayed in my head, "The watermelons will be ripe, and you will not eat them; there will be thousands of turtle eggs, and you will never taste them." Through the months of writing the thesis on hunting and distribution and its effects on social structure I remembered my dream the night I stayed in Esperanza waiting for the plane to leave the Purús. In my dream Ndaishiwaka lifted the *mosquitero* and said "Fando, I will not leave you."

When I returned to Marcos in the summer of 1968 the village seemed like a familiar home. Ndaishiwaka said he had dreamed I would come in June, and shaman's dreams are predictive. This was the second stage of my relationship with the Sharanahua. This is the romance of fieldwork.

Romance is a form of insanity in which one projects onto another a response to needs unmet and ignores the reality of the other person. The romance of fieldwork is no exception, where needs unmet in our own society for feeling connected to a group of people and experiencing a direct sensation of the physical environment lead one to romanticize primitive life. It is an anthropological mood: the despair of alienation in a cold world which seems doomed to progress only further into dehumanization casts a golden light on the deep greens of the Amazon Basin and one envisions the direct earthly satisfactions of hunting in order to eat, weaving so as to lounge in a hammock, painting one's face in order to make love. Just as the delusions of romance may be the only way in which it is possible for two people to justify the attempt to get to know one another, the romantic view of the field throws the anthropologist into an interaction with his people.

In this stage the Sharanahua were no longer objects of my study but were intensely a part of my life, so that social pressure structured most of my days. Although my command of the language was still at the level of a backward six year old, communication was easy, and I often felt part of the village. I responded correctly, that is in Sharanahua style, to many interactions and knew how to get what I wanted without saying a word. Taking part in the life of a small village in which day after day one interacts with the same small group of people and a multitude of clues makes it difficult not to know what anyone is feeling; one's daily moods become the reflection of those around you. Day follows day; the sun hurts, the three-day *frio* sends colds and coughs. We all go fishing and ecstatically eat and eat roast fish, boiled fish, and beautifully steamed manioc. Everyone gets drunk on raw cane liquor that the traders sell, and I spend too much and am sick drunk on a clear, hot morning, while traders coax ocelot skins from drunken men at crooked prices.

My field notes were thin much of that summer, and I often wished to throw them away. I wanted to be a Sharanahua and seriously thought of never leaving, but staying always to savor the beauty of the tropical forest, the coolness of bathing in the river in the late afternoon, then sitting with a cup of coffee on the steps of my house, watching the sun go down across the Purús river, behind Iconahua's plantain garden.

At the end of that summer, Bashkondi and I wept; Zacharais said, "Poor Fando, she must go back to her cold country"; Yawandi and Ndaishiwaka gave me gifts with no thought for a return present. I stayed with a friend in Lima for two weeks, considering whether to return to New York or to Marcos. Friends would have cared for my two children; jobs are replaceable; and though at times I have regretted the decision to leave then and not stay longer, in the end the same decision would have been made. I realized that I had been living in the best of two worlds. My participation as a woman in Sharanahua society was limited. I was neither able nor willing to fully learn the skills or endure the hard physical labor of my friends at Marcos. Also, I felt free at times to engage in conversations with men, to observe and finally participate in the drug ritual that is forbidden to Sharanahua women. The emotional ties to people at Marcos were real, but I could not accept the limitations that went with full membership in the society. I returned to Marcos once more, the summer of 1969, trying with little success to maintain more of a distance to protect myself from the sadness I had experienced upon leaving the year before. It was a difficult summer. I accomplished a great deal of work; I was often angry; and I knew as did my friends that I would leave the Purús.

My friends at Marcos were honestly involved with me, but this involvement was based on my ability to move in a world outside their own, to have things they could not buy, to listen with interest to thoughts that one does not share with other Sharanahua. They, too, feel restricted by their own society; its contradictions and limitations lead them to romanticize and envy others who seem less bound than themselves. When we travel to Esperanza, the Peruvian town where the plane lands, I see a wretched place, its few inhabitants unsatisfied, frustrated, seeking power and objects forever unavailable in the tropical forest, whereas Marcos seems a haven, a remnant, an oasis of beauty in an obsessive, over-populated anxious world. The Sharanahua, however, are fascinated by Esperanza. They are frightened of and repelled by Peruvians, but they visit this Peruvian town not only to trade skins and buy manufactured objects, but, as they say, "to look at Peruvians." Young men dress to look Peruvian and long for watches and sunglasses, even though when they strive to look their best at Marcos, their white shirts are set off elegantly by elaborate red or black face paint designs.

Through analyzing the data I collected in the field and by attempting to convey in this book the reality that is Marcos, I have reached a third stage in my relationship with the Sharanahua. This third stage of ethnography then is to see oneself in the primitive and the primitive in oneself, to open one's eyes to the restrictions that determine primitive life and to acknowledge that we too are restricted. This view leads to an understanding and respect for the Sharanahua's desire for Peruvian things and ways. It is not that who they may become, if in several generations they are acculturated, will be better. It is not that Peruvian or our own society is superior to theirs. It is a respect for humans drawn to transcend the limits of their society, as we may be driven to transcend ours. In writing this ethnography, therefore, I am attempting to describe the structures, the organization of social interactions, that provide the Sharanahua with an ongoing, relatively secure way of life; the contradictions and limitations produced by these structures; and the ways in which these shape the Sharanahua encounters with the world outside their own society.

In collecting and analyzing the data of the field both my training and the Sharanahua led me to study hunting and the distribution of meat. Meat seemed to be the main preoccupation of most people at Marcos as it also became mine. It fit with my training which assumed that subsistence and survival were the basic determinants of the structures of any society, and that if one wished to understand how and why a society works one should begin by considering first how any group's behavior may be related to solving the problems of existence.

Tropical forest Indian societies such as the Sharanahua's achieve a secure food supply through a way of life tightly bound to subsistence. One eats well at Marcos, but day in and day out one is preoccupied with the food quest. The Sharanahua also take part in activities unconnected with subsistence. They are concerned with other thoughts and other interactions. The dominance of subsistence activities, however, is observable in everyday life; and kinship rules, decisions as to marriage and residence, reflect or are colored by this dominance. The problems of survival structure the cultural rules of behavior, and social interactions are limited to provide security in an uncontrollable world.

Social interactions are the raw data of the ethnographer.

He participates in and observes them, looking for patterns, and asks, "Why did you do this?" "Why did someone else do that?" Most answers are norms, the approved, cultural reasons—"I gave meat to Tomuha because she is my mother's brother's wife." Some answers are indicative of cultural ideals—"We give meat to everyone." Both answers are informative, neither answer is true. They are not lies, no one is deliberately distorting the truth, but they do not match the observable patterns of behavior. Occasionally one does give meat to one's mother's brother's wife, but more often one does not. In the example given here, meat was not given to two other people who were also wives of mother's brothers. Although many people told me that at Marcos meat is given to everyone, in ten months I never found it to happen.

What people say is important, true or not, since it provides information on the expectations and obligations that are as much a part of the culture as the actual observable behavior. People are able to tell you their beliefs about their own society, and in no society does belief match observable reality. In some areas of social life, belief and reality are congruent; in many areas of social life they are contradictory. The most ardently held cultural beliefs are likely to be those that are most contradictory since they are continually challenged by perceptions and experiences that invalidate them. Ideology, particularly myths, reinforces these beliefs. They are a mold into which the evidence contradictory to the cultural beliefs may be shaped into apparent rationality, providing motivation —in heaven if not on earth—for the socially essential behavior.

Sharanahua society is secure and successful, but most interactions are laden with mutual obligations, and most interactions are restricted to kin. One's kin are in the Sharanahua language literally "my flesh," the only people one can ever depend upon. Yet the small child, jumping and splashing naked in the puddles of the rainy season with a bunch of other brown bodies, has learned that it is humans, not just kin, who are delightful. This knowledge will be buried soon by the lessons of Sharanahua culture, and the obligations of sharing every morsel of food with a brother and sister and of caring for a younger sibling will partly erode the pleasures of companionship even with kinsmen.

Myth and ritual give momentary expression to these unthinkable experiences, to the interactions pushed out of everyday awareness by the ongoing expectations and limits of social life. In myth and ritual one discovers the desires that the Sharanahua fear, experiences not congruent with the security of Sharanahua culture. The jaguar, the anaconda, the spirits of Sharanahua myths are symbolic images focusing multiple meanings, shifting and being transformed as they appear in different settings. A dreamer using these symbols seizes upon a fragment of the meaning to express a personal paradox or momentary dilemma. The men taking part in ritual are terrified or ecstatic as the spirits of myth appear before them. The shaman curing his patient informs this communication with the shared symbols of myth.

When Ndaishiwaka, after months of work, explained for the first time how a shaman uses his patient's dreams to effect a cure, he himself had a dream, which he told me a few days later. He had a dream that he and another man were taking *ayahuasca,* the drug that is used for ritual and curing, when they heard and saw an owl. Ndaishiwaka said, "That's my cousin, the spirit of *ayahuasca.*" The other man said, "You lie, it's not spirit cousin." Ndaishiwaka wanted to kill the owl; it was taking *ayahuasca* and was angry. It had the musical instrument of the *ayahuasca* spirits, guitar-like, made from a turtle shell. Then Ndaishiwaka was playing the instrument, and the *ayahuasca* spirit said angrily, "Don't play it, it's mine." Ndaishiwaka said, "You lie, it's mine." The spirit was angry and flew away.

The owl appears in one Sharanahua myth as the wise creature of the night, who warns the other animals of danger.

As in many other cultures, the owl at times stands for the shaman himself. The shaman sings when he cures to call the spirits, and though the tortoise-shell instrument is no longer made, it represents the singing, the knowledge, that Ndaishiwaka was sharing. In this dream Ndaishiwaka fought his own doubts about the wisdom of his decision to share shamanistic knowledge, trying to prove that it was his to give, and that in giving he would still have it.

When Ndaishiwaka told me this dream, we had been for several days in a somewhat confused and uncomfortable interaction concerning a shotgun. He had asked me to buy a shotgun for him, for which he gave me an ocelot skin. It was an exorbitant price for a skin, but I thought of it in part as payment over and beyond the usual informant gifts for unusual and valuable data. Although Ndaishiwaka had asked for the gun, the dream implied to me that he felt trapped by the obligation involved in accepting an extravagant gift. I explained then the value of his knowledge to me by saying that someday I would write a book, and by so doing would make up the amount of money I had paid for the shotgun. Therefore, he did not owe me anything.

Dreams are as elusive as myths, and their messages are many layered. I believe I interpreted Ndaishiwaka's dream with some accuracy, and the tension between us seemed relaxed. Working in a strange culture one finds moments of clarity as well as the days of confusion in which one understands language, but not meaning. To understand Sharanahua myths is to understand Sharanahua meaning, and there are myths that I find totally opaque—unresponsive to analysis, unenlightened by my experience of interactions with the Sharanahua. While I hope that some other anthropologist will carry my analysis further, one cannot wait for perfect knowledge. The Sharanahua taught me a good deal of their lives and culture and, as in the dream of the shaman, by sharing what I have learned I can better understand any culture, its security, its contradictions, and its limitations.

SHARANAHUA

Their Location, Their Culture, and Their History

Marcos is located on the Upper Purús River twenty miles west of the Brazilian border in the Department of Loreto in Peru. Until airplane service by the Peruvian government and missionary planes entered this region in 1953, the shortest route for an outsider was at least a month's journey, starting at Manaus and traveling up the Amazon to the mouth of the Purús and then continuing up the Purús into Peru. Nowadays to get to Marcos one travels by plane to Pucallpa, the boom-town of the Peruvian forest, which has been steadily expanding since 1943 when the road from Lima connected the forest, the *selva*, with the coast.

Pucallpa lies at the eastern foot of the Andes. Ten minutes after the plane has begun its descent from towering brown mountains with patches of green marking cultivated land and tiny clusters of villages seemingly dropped onto these heights, one is out over the green of tropical forest and drops to the hot humidity of the dusty Pucallpa airport. In 1966 the streets were just beginning to be paved and sewers were not yet ready to replace the open ditches.

Most of the population of Pucallpa are *selváticos*, born in Iquitos or the small river towns, starting in Pucallpa with a small stall or wagon, selling needles, scissors, cloth, flash-lights, batteries, mirrors, trying to save for a small store with double the inventory. A few have turned such stores into large businesses like Casa Sisley or Casa Choy Sanchez and have built hotels, arranged franchises to sell Fords, invested in airlines. These families visit Lima and Europe and send their sons to the national university to become lawyers or doctors. Most people in Pucallpa, however, have no knowledge of, or connection with, the coast or highlands of Peru. Many are poor, barely keeping their families in clothing and food.

Pucallpa is a jumping-off point into the forest for traders, missionaries, and anthropologists, and from the forest it is an entry to urban life where Indians learn to drop their own language and raise their children on *selva* Spanish. The plane trip from Pucallpa southeast across the forest to the Upper Purús is only two to three hours, but the frontier town of Esperanza is a lifetime away, back to fur traders and kerosene lanterns, while the Indian villages are another world entirely.

The Peruvian government subsidizes old DC-3s that fly twice a month from Pucallpa to Esperanza. A couple of passengers take this trip—a young woman visiting her fiancé who has a year's assignment to maintain the radio station in Esperanza; a trader whose stock of goods to sell fills the center of the plane. For most of the flight the view is of varying shades of green with an occasional yellow crown rising out of the canopy, the rivers, a few small clusters of thatched roofs, and garden clearings. Esperanza is no different, forty or so thatched roofs and the tin roofs of the priest's house and the radio shack.

The plane has barely stopped moving when children cluster around its wheels, and everyone in Esperanza crowds to receive mail or packages from the outside world or to see what other people are receiving. The three traders send men to take their cargo out of the plane, and the co-pilot orders any Indian in sight to help move the cartons and bags.

Reloading is rapid since the pilot wants to sleep in Pucallpa and even a brief rain will soak the grass landing strip and keep the plane in Esperanza. Stinking rolls of peccary skins, jaguar, and ocelot are thrown into the plane, large turtles are put inside on their backs with their legs tied. People ask the pilot and radio man or any passengers to take out mail or a small package to relatives in Pucallpa.

This airline, Civico, is the only link between the Peruvians in Esperanza and what they consider the real world. In the rainy season, starting in November and lasting till April, there are few planes. Sometimes two months go by and flights scheduled cannot land as the almost daily rains soak the grass field or the plane turns back as the sky piles high with black clouds. The traders look grim—nothing to sell, and no flour, canned milk, oil, or kerosene for their own houses. On the days the plane is due, the traders cluster around the radio shack and pressure the operator to assure Pucallpa that the weather is clear and fine, despite the suspicion of gray moving along the horizon from the west.

Esperanza is a frontier border town. The border is a reality to the foreigner whose visa limits him to either the Peruvian or Brazilian side. It is a partial reality to Peruvians and Brazilians who travel the river to trade and shift from Spanish to Portuguese as they enter Brazil or reverse as they cross back into Peru. The Spanish of these backwoods is as distant from the Spanish of Lima as the life of the traders in Esperanza is from the life of an urban storekeeper. This Spanish has many Portuguese sounds as well as a sprinkling of regional vocabulary.

For the Indians the border scarcely exists. Many are aware that Brazilians are different from Peruvians, that Portuguese is different from Spanish, that the Peruvian *sol* is not the Brazilian *cruzeiro,* but the Indians are neither Peruvian nor Brazilian. No official bothers to regulate the canoes that travel the Upper Purús; no fence divides Brazilian forest from Peruvian forest.

From Esperanza one travels most easily by water, downriver to Brazil, upriver in Peru. In the rainy season, when the Upper

Purús rises fifteen to twenty feet, the current hurls tree trunks and branches, and canoes travel close in to shore. In the dry season the water drops, exposing sandy beaches on the inner shore of each snake-like curve of the river, and at some spots one can walk across the river. Only shallow-bottomed craft can travel the Upper Purús during these months of low water —dugout canoes, laboriously poled up the river and swiftly paddled down or dugouts with *peque-peques,* the Peruvian motor boats with a long-handled tiller attached to the rudder so that the entire rudder can be lifted clear of a sunken log or a sudden shallow.

Traveling upriver from Esperanza, heading toward Marcos, for a half mile there are Indian houses along the banks, with clearings behind them edged by the forest. A mile upriver, and there are nothing but sand beaches with small sandpipers hopping their length, then low-growing cane and small trees, then a rising bank with the incredible soaring trees, a flock of green parakeets sounding like a rattle shaken.

The first village, Conta, is about three miles upriver from Esperanza. It consists of some six large households of Cashinahua, recent migrants from Brazil. Five miles further up the river is Piquinique, a Mastinahua village of three huge open houses set back on a fairly high bank. Another five miles of the repeated long, slow curve, high trees, sand beach, low scrub, blue sky, burning sun, cool water, then Canto Gallo with two families of Marinahua and one of Sharanahua. Five miles further to Flor de Mayo, deserted Yaminahua houses on the high bank, one tall lightning-blackened bare tree, standing high above the plantain gardens. On the low bank opposite, a single Sharanahua household still remains. A couple of other individual households of Sharanahua, and then Zapote—downriver three deserted houses, almost overgrown, which a few years ago belonged to Sharanahua who now live at Marcos.

The main village of Zapote is further upriver and looks very different from every other village on the Upper Purús. It is a Culina village with one large house for the headman and small, ten by ten feet, houses scattered around it. The Culina are the only group in this region whose language is totally different from that of the other groups.

Another five miles, three hours of poling a canoe, and one reaches Marcos. The Sharanahua say, "We are at Marcos," long before the houses are in sight since the beaches, the river, the streams, lakes, and forest are as much a part of the village as the houses that shelter people. The beaches are planted each spring with quick-growing crops, when the Purús recedes. In this dry season one searches the beaches each day for the tracks of large water turtles and uncovers the holes in which they have layed fifty to a hundred eggs. The river provides water for drinking, cooking, and bathing, and along with streams and the lake that lies a half-hour's walk behind the houses, provides fish, from the tiny shrimp that women gather to the giant *paiche* whose scales can bend the quarter-inch nails of a fishing spear. Near Marcos the forest is still abundant with game, though men must walk further to find it than they did the first year they came to Marcos. Peccaries occasionally run through the village settlement, causing intense excitement as everyone grabs shotguns, machetes, bows and arrows and goes crashing through the bushes in pursuit despite the real danger that the animals may attack. Monkeys and wild birds are the most numerous game; deer, capybaras, pacas, agoutis, and tapirs are often taken.

The forest is the source of land for gardens, trees bearing nuts, wild fruits, honey, and edible fungi. It provides wood for canoes, houses, spears, bows and arrows, mortars and pestles, stools, cooking fires, thatch for roofs, baskets, fire fans, and mats; and a large variety of plant fibers for hats and ropes for a multitude of purposes. Every piece of material for construction can be obtained from the forest.

As one travels up the river, one sees a few houses above the left bank and the reddish dirt of the ports, the cleared areas interspersed with green vegetation. The canoe is made fast with a vine to a pole stuck deep into the mud bank and, walking up a cleared trail and through the plantain garden, one arrives at one of the houses set back from the river. In 1966 only Julio's house was directly on the riverbank. The other row of seven houses were back on the higher ground behind the plantains. Five new houses have been built since then, also along the bank. Since everyone goes to the river several times a day to bathe and get water for cooking, there appears to be some advantage to being close to the water. An unusually high flood, however, may severely damage the houses, and there are also more gnats and mosquitoes near the river than near the forest.

The houses at Marcos are built high, the floors are four to six feet above the ground. One enters a house by climbing a notched stair pole, which at night is kicked away to prevent chickens and dogs from bothering the sleepers or littering the house. The raised floors are essential in the rainy season when the ground turns to puddles and mud. A shallow lake forms in the low ground of the plaintain gardens which lie between the raised riverbank and the main row of houses. Children shed their clothes and paddle old canoes back and forth between the trees.

Only from an airplane flying over Marcos can one see the entire village at once: the brown river on one side, two relatively parallel rows of houses, two or three clustered together in a clearing and separated from the rest by plantain gardens and scrub; on the inland side a stretch of overgrown former gardens, then the high green forest cover. From the ground one only sees a short distance before the scrub or gardens block one's view.

Each house, whether near or far from the river, has a path cleared to its own port, where the men keep their canoes, the women wash clothes and fetch water, and several times a day the household members bathe. On the other side of the house there is a cleared trail leading into the forest behind it, along which men leave to hunt and women to gather.

A separate cooking house is placed usually at right angles to the main house. The cookhouse has neither flooring nor walls, only a roof and a shelf to store plantains, bananas, corn, peanuts, pots, and fire fans. Wood fires for cooking are placed on the ground in the cookhouse and are thus protected from the rain. The cleared area around the house is carefully maintained by digging up the slightest hint of vegetation with a machete. It is said that keeping it cleared keeps away snakes, mice, and insects. Women sweep this area each day as part of their daily cleaning of the house.

On the inland side of these clearings, most households plant a bush of cayenne pepper and grow *huaca* and *barbasco* which are used for drugging fish. Next to the house of one of the older men are several small shrubs whose leaves are used as medicine.

The houses of Marcos are built in the same style as Peruvian houses in the forest, but the Sharanahua's are larger than the typical Peruvian's house in Esperanza. Some houses are walled with bark to give protection from the driving rains, some are left open. These houses take about two months to build. The most difficult part is to assemble the materials and to sink the heavy vertical poles straight and deep into the ground. The basic tool for this work as for all other construction at Marcos is the machete. As time passes additional walls may be added, and occasionally some inner partitions of bark are tied between narrow split bamboo strips to separate sleeping from eating areas or a young couple from the wife's parents.

From the outside, gray thatched roofs and bark walls look shabby or rundown, but on the inside, the careful workmanship is evident in the high roof with clear lines of thatch, poles of different dimensions selected for specific placement and weight bearing. At night, cloth *mosquiteros* are let down, large enough to stand in, within which a man's woven hammock or a woman's string hammock swings. Since women sleep with infants, it is more comfortable to let a baby urinate through the openings in a string hammock or wet two or three strands rather than soaking the tight cloth of the woven hammock.

In the morning *mosquiteros* are tied up to a rafter or in back of a hammock. Rafters and thatch provide the storage space. Shotguns, bows and arrows, machetes, and knives are pushed into the thatch which holds them firmly and keeps them dry. Baskets of braided fibers hang from the rafters holding balls of spun cotton, extra clothing, small pieces of beeswax for mending arrows, a piece of laundry soap, a jar of red face paint. Young men keep small cardboard suitcases, two hands long with a lock, in which personal valuables are kept: a belt, a white shirt, two or three shotgun shells.

The floor of the house is bare of furnishing except for a low stool carved to look like a turtle, and women sweep the floor after every meal. The small cracks between the lengths of heavy bark flooring make it simple to sweep any small bits of food or seeds or to spit to the ground below.

Several households keep a few chickens and ducks for sale to the traders who pass by the village. Every household owns innumerable dogs, emaciated and wormy. Some are hunting dogs, but most serve only to raise an alarm as one approaches a house. If one walks through the village at night, at every house a bunch of dogs yelps and growls, and one can enter only with a raised stick or a handful of stones to throw.

In 1966 there were eighty-nine people at Marcos, forty-four adults and forty-five children. By 1969 twelve more children had been born, four families had moved to Marcos from other villages, and there had been no deaths. At present the population is clearly expanding. Not everyone at Marcos is a Sharanahua. In 1966 the village included two Amahuaca, four Mastinahua, eight Yaminahua, four Chosinahua in addition to the seventy-one people at Marcos who identified themselves as Sharanahua.

The name "Sharanahua" means "good people," and it is the name they prefer, though other groups along the river occasionally call them "Pisinahua," "stinking people" or group them with the "Marinahua," "agouti people." It is tempting to refer to these named groups as tribes. It gives the illusion of a neat and organized category, a group of people around whom one may draw a boundary and for whom one might discover a history. Some groups, such as the Cashinahua, have a language distinct from that of other people, and they more readily fit into this category. Others, such as the Sharanahua, seem hardly more than a cluster of kinsmen sharing a name and speaking the same language as other small groups of kinsmen.

The people at Marcos dress for the most part in Peruvian-style clothing. Men wear shirts and slacks, women wear a single style of cotton dress, which they make from the insipidly patterned cheap cloth purchased from traders. Under their dresses, however, women still wear the traditional woven skirt. In the evening, returning from their bath in the river, they usually put away their dresses and wear only this skirt.

Men, women, and children paint their faces, women most frequently, usually with geometric designs. The paint is either red achiote, which lasts only a day and smears easily or black genipa, which stays clear and distinct for five days before beginning to fade. Women sometimes blacken their teeth for beauty, and all women remove their eyebrows and any body hair. Men keep their hair short like Peruvians, and women cut theirs in heavy bangs and to shoulder length. Older men and women past twenty have had their noses and lower lips pierced, and a few people still insert beads and metal ornaments. Women collect bead necklaces, wearing as many as possible and decorate their arms and ankles with beads.

For the most part the rhythm of life at Marcos is repetitive, rain or sun, an occasional three-day cold spell, then a few days of mild temperature, then oppressive heat. Cool mornings, hot afternoons and a million gnats, a half-hour's relief as the sun starts to set before nightfall brings a sky of stars and an attack of mosquitoes. Occasionally a man will sing at daybreak,

Bashkondi with fresh genipa face paint

a song of longing for a girl in another village. Women sing late in the afternoon in rhythm with the swing of a hammock lulling a baby to sleep. These songs are of fathers or brothers far away. A few times a week men chant through the night, drunk on a strong hallucinogenic.

Remnants of old dances appear a few times a year, when boys stomp in a circle, chanting the names of groups: "Marinahua, Chosinahua, Cashinahua, he, he, he, he, Sharanahua, Yaminahua, Fichinahua, he, he," or women form a circle, hands on each other's shoulders, and slowly dance as boys rush in teasingly to pull hair and to mimic. Now and then a trader staying at Basta's house brings a radio or a guitar, and young men and women hold each other awkwardly to dance in Peruvian style.

Twenty-five years ago Sharanahua men wore only belts under which they tucked their penises, a woven cotton shirt, and, on top of their long hair, hats made of a circle of ocelot or jaguar skin or of fiber decorated with strips of brightly painted straw. Women danced in hats of brilliant yellow and red toucan and macaw feathers or wore circlets of white or black tufts.

In the past twenty-five years many things have changed in Sharanahua life, though much has remained of the past. Although history and memory fade quickly losing the past under the Amazon's green forest and shifting rivers, Sharanahua culture undoubtedly changed in the past as well. Language itself documents some change—not only the shifts in meaning which are still remembered, but the shape of words and the sounds themselves. The many groups who speak closely related Panoan languages are clearly descendants of populations who shared a single language. Over the thousand years that it is estimated that these descendants each went its own way, the languages have changed so that a Shipibo cannot understand Sharanahua nor a Sharanahua "hear" an Amahuaca, even though a vocabulary from each group lists dozens of similar words. Over time one would assume that many other aspects of culture have changed, improved, were borrowed from a neighboring group, were lost, disappeared, or were replaced. The Sharanahua have only recently learned to make canoes, for if their ancestors understood this art, it had certainly been forgotten. In Sharanahua, the word for canoe, shasho, is the same as the word for mortar, both being made of hollowed-out solid trees. Other Panoan groups, such as the Shipibo, have a distinct word for canoe, noti, which is never used by the Sharanahua. The Shipibo are a numerous people who live along the flood plain of the Ucayali, a river dwarfed only by the Amazon itself.

Perhaps large groups such as the Shipibo-Conibo of the Ucayali have developed and elaborated techniques and knowledge from the simpler methods of the Sharanahua and other forest dwelling Panoan-speakers, such as the Cashinahua and Amahuaca; or perhaps the Sharanahua's forefathers were pushed from a more settled life and forced to relinquish and eventually failed to teach the ensuing generations the use of canoes, harpoons, and elaborate ceramics.

The transmission of technical knowledge and skills is not dependent upon a shared language, and over time groups living next to one another in similar ecological niches resemble one another culturally in many ways. Thus, the bows and arrows of the Upper Purús are distinct from those of the Ucayali, regardless of the languages spoken by their makers. The Arawak-speaking Culina and the Panoan-speaking Sharanahua of the Upper Purús have as much or more in common than the Sharanahua and the Shipibo. Over many generations, cultures emerging from the people and the forest have developed into various ways of life, different yet similar in their smooth fit to the forest and rivers of the Amazon.

In the Amazon Basin, land and water change as rivers find new channels, pile silt to form new banks, leave behind oxbow lakes—a piece of the curve of the river that has become landbound. Peruvian towns built as permanent ports find themselves high and dry, while Indian villages moving faster than the changes are always near a convenient stream or river. The next piece of forest will have the same woods and bamboos for construction, the same game to hunt, fish to catch, land to clear for gardens. No concentration of a single species of trees makes one part of the forest more valuable than the next, no distinct herds of animals utilizing a unique vegetation encourages hunters to pick one acre against the next.

Yet the forest is not as homogeneous as the endless tree canopy and the repetition of animal species implies. A hunter may note the difference in increased abundance of animals near certain rivers or avoid a stream where gnats and mosquitoes are particularly voracious. An agriculturalist may seize on the rich, silt-laden banks of one river, passing by the clear waters of another stream. Rubber gatherers finding better spoils in some forest regions left others unravaged. The Amazon Basin varies over time and space in relation to the needs and skills of the populations who have dwelt there. Its first human inhabitants were probably small groups of hunters and gatherers, who exploited the river banks for turtles and turtle eggs, fish, and aquatic mammals; the forest for nuts, fruits, edible fungi, honey; vines for drugs; barks for cloth, decoration, medicine; and materials for manufactures. Spears may have been the earliest weapons of these hunters, but bows and arrows, wherever and whenever invented, not only increased the range and thrust of men as predators, but added to their resources the monkeys and birds of the high canopy. Until the invention of the canoe and harpoon, small streams were easier to fish with bow and arrow or fishing spear than large rivers.

The date and place where plants were first domesticated in the tropical forest is still unknown, but agriculture is an important part of the subsistence of most Indian cultures. Manioc is probably the earliest crop domesticated by tropical forest peoples. It is the most important staple crop of the Amazon and has been adopted throughout the world in tropical regions. It is an incredibly sturdy plant, needing only a small amount of rainfall and ideally at least a year to grow. It is better after a year and a half and may be left in the ground until needed for another year. Manioc must be planted in well-drained soil, so that flood plains and other low-lying areas that may be even temporarily inundated are not desirable.

The domestication of maize and peanuts, however, reverses the preference for higher ground. Since both plants grow rapidly within the boundaries of a single dry season, the ever-renewed shores of the rivers draining the Andes emerged as a desirable and distinct ecological niche. Not every large river in the Amazon Basin builds a fertile flood plain. Those draining from the ancient soils of the Brazilian and Guiana shields, the oldest portion of the continent, for the most part bring little fresh soil along their paths, while the geologically recent upthrust of the Andes provides new soils to the silt-heavy rivers that flow down their eastern slopes into the forest.

Samuel fishing along the lake shore

Bananas and plantains are currently believed to have come to the Amazon with the entry of Europeans. They are now ubiquitous in the tropical forest. They are tolerant of swampy land and can produce for years, so that they provide a mode of utilizing land difficult to exploit with either manioc or maize.

Agriculture alone cannot provide all of the necessary elements of diet since none of the crops grown in the tropical forest are sufficiently rich in protein. There were no easily domesticated animals in this region, but game and fish provide the essential proteins.

In terms of the ways in which the Indians of the tropical forest exploit their resources, it is possible to discern two ecological niches and two ways of life in the Amazon Basin: the interfluvial and the riverine. Interfluvial societies, such as the Sharanahua, exploiting small streams for fish and depending primarily on hunting as their protein source, tend to be small groups, moving their settlements frequently since these resources are easily exhausted. Game is the factor which determines population density, settlement size, and the duration of time a settlement may remain in the same place. The small size of these groups leaves agricultural land plentiful. New gardens may be cleared each year and used plots left to fallow for twenty or more. Despite the thin soils of the interfluvial regions this type of utilization leaves almost no scars. Considering the generations of people who have lived in the Amazon forest and their semi-nomadic style of life, there is probably not a single square foot of the Amazon Basin that has not at one time or another been cultivated, yet in areas far from European settlement, such as the Upper Purús, one sees climax vegetation, the full potential of the forest released, perhaps, for the last time in the history of our planet.

The invention of the dugout canoe opened the large rivers and lakes—an incredibly rich source of fish. Indian groups with the technical knowledge to fish the rivers and the lakes have an abundant source of protein. Their settlements tend to be larger and more permanent. Their increased numbers make it necessary to utilize land differently, to take advantage of the flood plains of the rivers.

The Sharanahua have begun to learn to adapt to living along the banks of a large river. Settlement along the Upper Purús has shifted their relationship to their environment. The first and crucial step in adapting to this riverine environment was the selection of soil types appropriate to their crops. Twenty-five years ago the Sharanahua planted all crops in upland gardens far from the river. Today a basic division is made between flood plain and upland soils, between quick-growing crops and all others. Women plant quick-growing peanuts, maize, and watermelons at the beginning of the dry season in the freshly silted land behind the beaches of the Purús. These are harvested before the fall rise of the river. Men plant manioc in well-drained upland soils and set banana, plantains, and cane in land that is occasionally inundated at the height of the rainy season. Within the past ten years, the Sharanahua have learned to make canoes, which permits them to further exploit the fishing resources of the Upper Purús and to expand the range of hunting and available land for gardens. They have further learned to make harpoons and fish nets, which may lead to an increasing dependence upon fish rather than meat as the important source of protein.

The main reason for the Sharanahua settling directly along the banks of the Upper Purús was to have access to trade goods—either by traveling downstream to Esperanza or dealing with the traders who travel up the river in the dry season. Though the Upper Purús is still a backwater relatively unexploited by Peruvians, it is a large river along which influences and goods flow from the world outside.

Throughout the history of the Amazon the dominant society, Peruvian, Brazilian, Ecuadorian, or Colombian, has followed the pattern of expansion along the rivers. The more easily traveled waterways, the best land, the richest fishing areas are predominantly settled by these nationals rather than by Indians. The huge villages of Indians that the early explorers described have been replaced by river towns, poor by national standards and usually far smaller than the Indian villages they have replaced. Many of their inhabitants look like Indians but identify themselves with the national culture. Being an Indian is a way of life not a question of genetics. There are a few white Indians, and there are a multitude of Peruvians with features and coloring indistinguishable from the Sharanahua.

Near any Peruvian jungle town dust blows in the dry season, mud gluts the road in the rainy season. Land must be cleared of thick, impassible second growth, each few feet of clearing a terrible day's work of slow chopping with a machete. The myriad of turtles and turtle eggs no longer exist and are shipped as a luxury from areas still untouched. Game have vanished and cattle do poorly, further exhausting the land. Until recently the difficulty of communication has protected many of the interfluvial zones from this devastation, but the roads now breaking into the Amazon Basin, bringing colonists and settlements, will in all likelihood and with greater rapidity exhaust the fragile natural resources of the inland forests. Perhaps some technological leap will be devised to preserve resources for ensuing generations, but as yet European technology in the forest has not even equaled that of the Indian technology it replaces. On the whole, European culture, a way of life evolved on more enduring soils, has been a disaster to the tropical forest, entering what appeared a lush haven and leaving a desert of scrub.

Previous inroads into the hinterlands of the forest by Peruvian nationals has been in search of quick wealth: sarsaparilla, rubber, hardwoods, skins, depending upon the year and the world market. These were relatively brief interludes with no thought of colonization, destructive not to the land and its resources but to the inhabitants. The structure of the forest with a single resource dispersed widely but sparsely has flung these adventurers into contact with Indians near every navigable river throughout the *selva*. Wherever possible Indian labor has been coerced or bought to supply the products and to feed the invaders. Forced by threats and seduced into debt by European goods—shotguns, machetes, axes, and knives—Indians worked or fled further into the forest, were killed or died of new diseases to which they had no previous immunity. Like ripples spreading in a pond, the entry of a rubber trader or hardwood *patrón* spread new things to groups who never met a European.

Colonists settling along the rivers, and rubber barons raping the forest set off waves of migrations as Indians lost their lands or fled further inland, pushing in turn other Indian groups to seek uncrowded areas and more peaceful regions. Thus around 1900 the Sharanahua left the small streams of the interfluvial region near the headwaters of the Taruacá River in Brazil as other Indian groups began to crowd them, pushed in turn by Brazilian settlements and rubber workers along the main river.

By 1945, when the Sharanahua first settled near the Upper Purús in Peru, they found a river empty of Indian settlements, although in 1866 Chandless, an English geographer, had reported several *malocas,* large communal houses, along this stretch of the river. In the interval between Chandless' trip and the Sharanahua's entry, the rubber boom had entered this region. The forest shows no apparent scars nor traces of this brief enterprise, but the prior populations of Indian groups have vanished.

The Sharanahua carry the past with them, as all people do. Their past is not stored in books but in memories clouded by time and shadowed by the fear of the spirits of the dead, whose names should not be mentioned. The Sharanahua say that they were once numerous, that settlements contained two or three *malocas* that sheltered sixty to ninety people, that along the small streams draining into the Taruacá River there were many settlements of Sharanahua. Baiyakondi (Ndaishiwaka's father) says, "My land is the Taruacá." It is where his father lived when he was born, and the land to which his spirit will return when he dies. It was high land, and he recalls that his father planted peanuts in the gardens since they lived far from sandy beaches like those of the Purús.

In attempting to trace the Sharanahua's history, I found that at the time they say they were living near the Taruacá in the early 1900s, two geographers, Tastevin and Rivet, traveled extensively through the region. In their accounts of the Taruacá, the Muru, and the Embira rivers, they list an incredible number of tribes with names ending in *nahua,* "people." The Sharanahua are not listed as such, but references to Saianahua or Chananahua or Marianahua may refer to Baiyakondi's and Basta's fathers.

The Sharanahua are few today because of the population loss that followed their first exposure to new diseases. Grippe, measles, and whooping cough, invariably deadly to peoples with no prior immunity, wiped out whole families. One way of dating contact between Indians and nationals throughout the tropical forest is to find out when the first epidemics struck. The Sharanahua had traveled to the Upper Curanja River by about 1935. They had been attacked by Peruvians on the Yaminahua River and believed that the epidemic of grippe came from a bomb dropped by the Peruvians. They moved south, looking for revenge and trade goods. On the Curanja they had met one Peruvian who tried to steal Basta's wife, Yawandi's mother. Yawandi was then about three year's old and she remembers weeping for her mother. The Peruvian was killed and Basta's wife returned.

Samuel and Bashkondi were born on the Curanja, and Samuel remembers the last *maloca* and his envy of the superiority of the houses of Peruvians who had machetes, *mosquiteros*, and good clothing. The Sharanahua had seen machetes, axe heads, and steel knives before and had seized them from other groups back on the Taruacá, while they were raiding for women. At Curanja, they killed three Brazilians and a Peruvian trader, partly in revenge and partly to take trade goods.

Measles struck at Curanja and they moved again, this time to the Upper Purús where they fought the Yaminahua. They say that the Peruvians threatened to bomb them if they continued fighting and, few in numbers, they became civilized. The last deadly epidemic hit at Chuspi, a stream leading into the Upper Purús, and every family lost two or more children to whooping cough. These evil days are long ago, and the disorganization and terror of villages with death after death are not a usual topic of conversation, though the remnant of fear flares into current stories of Peruvians dropping bombs of grippe and measles. While it is impossible to know exactly the extent of the Sharanahua's loss, on the basis of their memories I would estimate that one-half to two-thirds of their people died between 1925 and 1950.

The Sharanahua are no longer numerous, only some ninety people use this name, though they say that perhaps there are

Basta heading for his canoe with a shotgun

more in Brazil near the Acre River. There is a tinge of sadness at being few. Basta says that at Marcos he and Baiyakondi are the only men alive of his generation, and Basta weeps over the impending death of Chicolopez at Flor de Mayo, saying that he is the last of my kin. The world seems small and closing in, and each regards his kin as a small island of strength, the loss of even one to be a personal danger. The wailing for a sick kinsmen is highly stylized, the dirge-like, "my child is dying, my child is dying," and it is fueled, perhaps, not by grief for a unique person, but rather for the danger of one more tree gone in a small grove, never to be replaced.

A few Sharanahua have left their own people and traveled with traders to the world outside, to Pucallpa, Iquitos, or Brazil. I saw one man stop at Marcos, briefly visiting before continuing downriver with his *patrón,* the trader for whom he worked. He had been gone for many years, and the women of his kin group ran to the bank to meet him, sank to the ground, holding his legs and wailing, "My child, my child has come." In the same way a baby, born into the group of kinsmen is greeted, and a kinsman leaving the Sharanahua's world is mourned as a man dying.

Samuel told a version of an origin myth, which seemed to reflect the occasional mood of being a small group of people in a world of strangers. A large basket opened, and all the groups of the world came out. Each group wore its own hats. The Sharanahua wore ocelot hats, other Indians wore feathers, and the Peruvians wore straw. There were great numbers of Peruvians, a few Sharanahua, and numerous groups of other Indians.

The plantain trees at Chuspi still bear fruit, and people still return to those gardens. Yet Chuspi was filled with the spirits of the dead, so fifteen years ago they moved to Camarú, downriver on the Upper Purús, where three of Ndaishiwaka's children, two of Basta's, and four of Zacharais' grandchildren were born. There were several additional moves during the past ten years to various sites on the Upper Purús, and Zacharais' and Basta's households parted from Baiyakondi's and Ndaishiwaka's as well as from others living then at Camarú. When villages are moved, they often split, and some close members of a kin group settle in one place, others remain or move elsewhere. Traveling along the river one may stop at another village and demand hospitality of one's kinsmen.

Marcos was begun in 1965 when an American missionary couple sought a new village after their home burned down at Boca de Curanja. A few Sharanahua households followed them from their old village; Basta, Zacharais, and Samuel left their relatively new homes at Zapote and built anew at Marcos. Baiyakondi had lived at Marcos before and he returned as did his sons, Ndaishiwaka and Iconahua. The missionary appears to counter the tendency for small groups to spread out along the river. A few years after the missionaries left Boca de Curanja those who had remained began to disperse, a few coming to Marcos, others settling further upriver in the opposite direction.

Marcos is becoming larger as additional families join the village. The Sharanahua's population is currently expanding. Each year the men at Marcos clear land and hunt further from the village. Most Sharanahua say that they plan to stay at Marcos. They want to remain within a couple of days' travel time to Esperanza. They like the missionary presence, which assures them of medicines and an exciting contact with the world by means of the missionary's radio and the airplanes that fly him in. They enjoy access to the missionary's trade goods, which usually cost less than the traders' stock.

Their cultural heritage is that of interfluvial hunters, and their society is still strongly focused on meat. To remain at Marcos this focus must shift since permanent settlement and population expansion will exhaust the game. If they remain at Marcos, fishing and agriculture will become more important than hunting, and many elements of their society will be transformed along with this shift.

Adapting to the riverine environment is well within the flexibility of the Sharanahua's methods of organizing their society; but if they move toward increasing interactions with Peruvians it will be on Peruvian terms, and these terms will shatter Sharanahua life. The Sharanahua still keep their distance from Esperanza and from Peruvians. They still maintain their social charter, a map of relationships that organized the old *malocas* as it organizes the village of Marcos.

3

MALOCA

The Plan of the Social Universe

"Listen, I will tell you," said Basta:

> In the darkness Moon made love to his sister. It was evening
> and he kept making love to her. She wondered who her lover
> was, so in the darkness she painted half of his face with black
> genipa. The next day she watched the men going along the
> path. Suddenly she saw the man, "No, it cannot be, it is my
> older brother who has genipa on one side of his face!"
>
> "May you die!" she said. "May a foreigner [nawa]
> kill you!" He ran from his angry sister, crying.
>
> Now, everyone left, and foreigners came killing his
> people. They fought, and his people ran away, but one
> man was hidden, and he cut off Moon's head. It was late
> afternoon, becoming dark, and there was no moon. The
> fire beetles were flying back and forth, and Moon took their
> excrement and put it on his head so that he too shone in
> the dark. Now the head went to the house, and his own
> people screamed, "Ari! a foreign ghost is coming!" and
> they fled.
>
> Then his older brother put the head in a basket.
> "Older brother, get me water," said the head.
>
> Older brother fetched water, but when the head drank,

the water dripped out of his neck. Then older brother left with his people and crossed the river, splashing, because the water was beginning to rise. The head went rolling, rolling after him. "Older brother," he said, "wait."

The people found palm fruit and ate all but one. "Older brother, throw down the fruit." But when he ate it, it fell through his neck, and he wanted to die.

His older brother ran on, and the head called, "Older brother, wait!" But his brother kept running. The foreign ghost was coming so he shut the house.

Now the head came rolling and cried, "Why did you shut the house? Open it, I want to go in." The head went round and round his mother's house.

"Mother, why did you close the house? Give me corn drink." From inside the house she gave him corn drink, but as he drank it, it dripped from his neck.

Then Moon told the people inside the house that there was a big armadillo on the trail. He was lying so that they would come out, and as they came, Moon made love to all the women. "Ari!" they screamed. "Why does my vagina bleed?"

Then Moon asked his mother for a black ball and a white ball of thread, which she threw from the house. Then Moon went up the thread to the sky, and all his people watched, and they said, "My child, my child goes playing to the sky."

Then many women, three days after he came, bled. One woman after another, all of them.

"Thus, my father told and long ago I listened to the story of Moon Spirit," said Basta.

To the children listening, lying on the floor, laughing by the kerosene lantern at Basta's dramatics, the house from which Moon is barred may be simply his mother's house. To Basta and to his father, the house was the *maloca,* a social world

from which the incestuous lover is forever banished. Every adult
over thirty year's of age has lived in a *maloca,* within which
people slung hammocks in two rows along the oval sides, with
cooking fires on the ground between. Samuel remembered it with
distaste, saying, "The floor was dirt, it was dark and smoky, we
had no clothes and no *mosquiteros,* and I had to stay inside
with my mother and kin." The next night Samuel dreamed that
he was back in the *maloca* and in his dream it was spacious
and beautiful.

The *maloca* in the myth of Moon and the *maloca* of
Samuel's dream can be interpreted as an image of order, a
bounded social world outside of which lies chaos. The Sharanahua occasionally use the term *"oni koi,"* "true people," when
they are comparing themselves with spirits, animals, or foreigners. It is a term used little in ordinary conversations, mainly
appearing in myths or rambling stories of the past to describe
a Sharanahua who encounters spirits in human or animal shape.
Oni koi is sometimes used in contrast to *"nawa,"* people who
are not considered humans, but more often *"noko kaifo"* "our
people," draws the boundary between those who are human and
those who are not. Occasionally in a myth *"noko pushu,"* "our
house," alternates with *"noko kaifo."* Outside this boundary
nothing is predictable, no social cues exist to distinguish safe
from dangerous. The friendly stranger who invites one to eat
may be a spirit hunting for human flesh or a foreigner plotting
murder.

Today the term *nawa* is applied only to Peruvians, strangely
powerful men, speakers of another language, eaters of disgusting
animals like cows, potential cannibals with enormous sexual
appetites. I once pointed out to Ndaishiwaka that the word
nawa appeared to be like the sound of Shara-nahua or Cashinahua, which he translated as "people." He was startled by
the coincidence and said that he had never noticed it.

The word *nawa* appears in many myths, but not to describe
Peruvians. Yawandi said that it referred to people like the

Culina, whose language is different from Sharanahua, who eat snakes and never bathe. In stories Amahuaca and Mastinahua are sometimes called *nawa,* although the Amahuaca language is closely related to Sharanahua, and Mastinahua speak the same language. It is said that the Amahuaca have huge penises and can kill a woman with sexual intercourse; the Mastinahua make love to their own sisters.

Usually the term *yura futsa,* "other people," is used to describe members of any other Indian group, so that most of the time Culina, Mastinahua, and Amahuaca are *yura futsa.* The words themselves, however, suggest that *yura futsa* once contrasted with *unwu yura,* "my kin." *Yura* means "flesh" or "people," *futsa* means "other" and, in an old usage, also means "brother." It seems likely that at some point in times these two categories, *yura futsa* and *unwu yura* were both included in the category of *noko kaifo.* In the past this category may have included only Sharanahua, and in the past, it is said that one might kill another Sharanahua and steal his wife, as long as he was not a member of *unwu yura.* In the past Chosinahua and Marinahua may have been *yura futsa or* even *nawa,* today they are usually included within *noko kaifo.* While chance and population numbers, alliances or enmities, shift the definition of who is included within these categories, the meaning, the implications of these categories appears more enduring. *Yura futsa* are people one may marry and with whom one takes on obligations. They obey incest taboos, they usually speak the language, they eat ordinary food. Yet, since they are not one's kinsmen they are distrusted. At Boca de Curanja it is said that *yura futsa* are always angry and fighting, men beat their wives, and the women spit at each other; the Yaminahua who used to live at Flor de Mayo are murderers. In contrast to *nawa, yura futsa* are distrusted for human qualities. Like us they lie, steal, and kill, but they do not commit incest or eat people.

The fear of *nawa* became overt during my first six months in the field, when a story traveled up and down the river, a type of story I discovered later, that is familiar to most anthropologists in the Amazon. It was said that a Peruvian trader told it. A sick Peruvian in Esperanza had been sent to a doctor in Pucallpa. The doctor had put the sick man in a machine which cut him open to take his grease. The grease would be used to make bombs.

At Basta's household the women told me they were frightened, and everyone talked about how young men's fat was yellow and better than old men's fat, and I became nervous about the tinned butter in my house and the jokes we had exchanged about canned frankfurters. Sixteen-year-old Koyo finally asked me, "Fando, do you eat people?" I denied it as calmly as I could and asked her the same question. We exchanged our views on what was and was not edible, and I felt she would not have asked if she had really feared me.

I was further reassured when Shandi stole my towel off the line and, in answer to Bashkondi's scolding, shrugged and said, "*Yura futsa*, why not?" I overheard this conversation since it would never have been said directly to me. No Sharanahua ever denies a kinship relationship directly or calls someone *yura futsa* to their face. Thus, when I asked Yawanini how she was related to Tarani, a young Yaminahua girl adopted into Basta's household, Yawanini did not reply. Tarani was standing next to us and knows Yawanini very well. Only after Tarani walked away, and I repeated my question did I receive the reply, "*yura futsa.*"

Today the Culina are *yura futsa*, but they are still treated partially like *nawa*. On a river trip we stopped at Zapote, the Culina village, and the Sharanahua men acted oddly, a mixture of politeness and contempt, not the way I had seen them behave in a Marinahua or Yaminahua village. Ishamba, a young married woman, never moved from my side, sitting close beside me as long as we stayed in the Culina village. At Flor de Mayo, the Yaminahua village, she joined the women in their cookhouse, and it was I who followed her for social support.

Another time as we stopped at Zapote, Yawandi urged her son to eat the meat a woman offered. The woman was a Sharanahua who had been taken by a Culina long ago. She was a distant relative of Yawandi's, who said to her son, "Waranamani, eat your mother's food." He refused and as we moved away said, "She's not my mother, she's a dirty Culina." Yawandi remonstrated with him, but she appeared insincere.

On first meeting, a group may be identified as *"nawa,"* but if the relationship continues, through marriages and in the past through alliances, they may become *yura futsa.* As time passes children are born and include these foreign fathers and mothers among their kin, so that they too will become *noko kaifo.*

It is tempting to assume that there was a time long ago, when generation of Sharanahua followed generation, according to some orderly, consistent, and stable pattern. One sees apparent disorganization in the present, with overlapping, inconsistent categories of identity and tries to reconstruct a golden age of order like the dream of the *maloca.* The Sharanahua inherit from the past the methods of dealing with the disorderliness of any present and create a secure universe in each generation.

Within the *maloca* ties were either of kinship or marriage. These ties regulated the essential work of the society: the division of labor, rights to land and hunting trails, obligations of help and support. There is only one role in Sharanahua society that is not based on a social position determined by kinship or marriage, and this is the shaman's role. All of the other social roles that make up Sharanahua society are divided and specified by the type of relationship that binds any two people.

As compared to the endless list of social roles in our society, Sharanahua society is extraordinarily simple in dividing up all social and economic relationships between eight roles. These are: *upa* (father and father's brothers), *uwa* (mother and mother's sisters), *achi* (father's sisters and potential mother-in-law), *koka* (mother's brothers and potential father-in-law), *poi* (sibling of the opposite sex), *futsa* (sibling of the same sex), *chai* (cousin of the same sex), *bimbiki* (cousin of the opposite sex). Women use the same terms as men with the exception of *yaya* in place of *achi* and *tsafu* in place of *chai*.

It is misleading to translate these words into English since neither the literal meaning nor the emotional significance is equivalent. A Sharanahua child knows the *uwa*, "mother," who bore him, even though his other *uwa*, "mother's sisters," may have cared for, nursed him, and rocked him to sleep. One *upa*, "father," is the man who conceived him and is married to his mother, but any one of his *upa*, "father's brothers," are men who will help provide for him until he is a man.

In English these are terms that imply unique personal relationships, in Sharanahua these are types or categories of people with whom one may or may not have a personal relationship but with whom one shares certain mutual obligations and rights.

In the closed world of the *maloca*, a child learned to distinguish these few different types of relationships. In Sharanahua one does not call kinsmen by their names; to do so is to deny any relationship. Every member of his parents' generation was an *upa*, an *uwa*, an *achi*, "father's sister", or a *koka*, "mother's brother." His siblings included far more people among the Sharanahua than is usual in our own kinship system. The sons and daughters of any of one's "fathers" or "mothers" are siblings; the sons and daughters of any fathers' sister or mothers' brother are cousins. Again, to translate into English is deceptive since neither sibling nor cousin carries the same meaning as the terms that the Sharanahua use. There is no term that is equivalent to sibling or brother or sister. In the past there were *poi* (sibling of the opposite sex) and *futsa* (sibling of the same sex). Nowadays the more commonly used terms are *ochi*, "older brother," *ursto*, "younger brother," *chipi*, "older sister," *chiko*, "younger sister." In terms of personal relationships, there may be a world of different feelings for the older sister who carried you and cared for you and an older sister with whom one occasionally played, a younger brother with whom one slept under one's parents' hammock or a distant younger brother tagging after the older boys. In terms of mutual obligations all brothers or sisters are the same, with different responsibilities accruing to older or younger.

To understand Marcos is to learn the kinship system since the structuring of every action one might call economic, social, or political is organized by the categories imposed upon those people to whom one is related. In our society kinship appears small in importance as the world is filled with thousands of occupations, social segments, governmental bodies, classes, ethnic groups, all of which are organized by many varying structures. In comparison the organization of life at Marcos is simple—all work divided only between the sexes, responsibilities and expectations allotted between eight or ten categories (eight if the older sibling terms are used, ten if the current sibling terms are used). Within the operating social world of the Sharanahua there are only eight possible social roles, eight different types of people.

The simplicity of the social structure appears truly foreign to an American and, therefore, complex. But it is not the foreign words for social roles that makes it difficult to explain kinship, it is that the explanation shakes the structure of our own thought. The problem in describing how the Sharanahua categorize the various humans of their society is that the analysis demonstrates the artificial, the socially agreed upon nature of these categories and thereby threatens our own since we believe, as the Sharanahua do, that our kinship system is biologically validated, eternally true. The Sharanahua say, "my kin, my flesh." We say or, if unsaid, believe "blood is thicker than water."

A Sharanahua accepts his kinship system as we do—it is real, it is true, and he learns as a child to expect certain kinds of behavior from certain kinds of kin. To the outsider a confusing feature of Sharanahua kinship is that terms alternate from generation to generation. Thus, a man calls to his small son, *"upa,* come here," and the son replies, "yes, *upa,* I'm coming." A child being taught how to address each of his kin can simply learn how to categorize his social universe by responding to how each adult addresses him. For a boy the rule is to call his male kin exactly what they call him, so that any man who calls him *upa* may be answered with the same term. In the same way, when the child becomes a man, he will call his own sons *upa.* A man who calls him *koka* is responded to as *koka.* Any woman who, like his own mother, calls him *koka* is responded to as *uwa,* and other women who call him *upa* are his *achi.*

The same rules apply for a girl. She calls any woman of her parents' generation exactly what they call her. A man who calls the girl *uwa* is her *koka,* a man who calls her *achi* is her *upa.*

The generations seem to alternate in this scheme so that the basic kinship categories include only two generations, one's own and one other. One's parents and one's children are in the other, and are, therefore, called *upa* or *uwa, achi* or *koka.* One's siblings and cousins are in one's own generation as are one's grandparents and grandchildren. The same terms are applied, therefore, so that father's father may be called *ochi,* "older brother" and son's son *ursto,* "younger brother." Naikashu calls her son Gustavo, *koka,* and logically calls his daughter *tsafu,* the woman's term for a cousin of the same sex.

Kinship categories are neither emotionally uncharged nor neutral. Since each kinship category involves a different set of appropriate social interactions, it is not surprising that desire is aroused by the flirtatious provocative interaction between all *bimbiki* and usually surpressed by the decorum and matter-of-fact support of, in the old term, *poi.* One, in our metaphor, "falls in love" with *bimbiki* because he or she elicits the response. The interaction between a man and any woman who is not forbidden by the incest taboo is one of mutual provocation or total avoidance. If one has no actual *bimbiki* unmarried or

Sharanahua terms of address

1. A male point of view:

They call me	I call them	Relationship category
upa	upa	father and father's brothers
koka	uwa	mother and mother's sisters
upa	achi	father's sisters, potential mothers-in-law
koka	koka	mother's brothers, potential fathers-in-law
futsa	futsa	my sex, children of all fathers and mothers
poi	poi	opposite sex, children of all fathers and mothers
chai	chai	my sex, cousins and potential brothers-in-law
bimbiki	bimbiki	opposite sex, cousins and potential spouses

2. A female point of view:

They call me	I call them	Relationship category
achi	upa	father and father's brothers
uwa	uwa	mother and mother's sisters
yaya	yaya	father's sisters, potential mothers-in-law
uwa	koka	mother's brothers, potential fathers-in-law
futsa	futsa	my sex, children of all fathers and mothers
poi	poi	opposite sex, children of all fathers and mothers
tsafu	tsafu	my sex, cousins and potential sisters-in-law
bimbiki	bimbiki	opposite sex, cousins and potential spouses

The current terms for siblings are used in the same way by males and females and include the children of all "fathers" and "mothers."

younger "brother" —ursto
younger "sister" —chiko
older "brother" —ochi
older "sister" —chipi

available, one marries outside of the kin group and calls one's spouse *bimbiki*. The preference, however, is for an actual *bimbiki* since having *koka* rather than a stranger as a father-in-law is as conducive to desire as the fact in our society that one's girl friend's father is wealthy.

Women say, "sister's child is my child," and freely nurse their sister's children, supporting thus their role as *uwa*, "mother." The relationship between a woman and her brother's children is different. She may carry them and play with them affectionately, as I have seen Bashkondi play with her small *upa*, Samuel's son, but she hands him back to his mother when he cries for the breast. Ndaishiwaka flirts with and teases his five-year-old *bimbiki*, but is solemnly affectionate to a distant daughter we encountered at Canto Gallo, praising her ability to make a basket.

The maintenance of all of these roles depends upon the incest taboo since marriage with a sister, however distant, muddies the line between father and mother's brother, mother and father's sister, brothers and cousins, sons and sons-in-law. It is the basic charter of the Sharanahua social world, morality laden, sanctioned by the universe itself in the myth of Moon.

When I heard the story of Moon again at Baiyakondi's house, his young granddaughters were told to cover their ears and leave when he came to the part where Moon makes love to all the women and they begin to bleed. I asked later why they had been sent away since any Sharanahua child able to talk has heard endless discussions of sex. Baiyakondi replied that the girls would begin to menstruate too young, if they listened.

Tundo, Baiyakondi's wife, laughed at the beginning and said, "Moon is a Mastinahua, the Mastinahua have intercourse with their sisters." The word she used for sister, *poi*, was the one that both Baiyakondi and Basta used in telling the story, explaining to me that it meant, "younger sister," *chiko*. Later, having heard this word used in several myths for men as well as women, I realized that it is best translated as "sibling of the opposite sex." It is the direct social contrast to *bimbiki,* "cousin of the opposite sex," the man or woman one should marry, and to confuse these two relationships, to have sexual intercourse with *poi* rather than *bimbiki* is to hopelessly upset the entire kinship map of social roles. A distant sister may be beautiful, but to marry *poi* would be to eliminate the very relationships that organized the life of the *maloca.*

The first few people who told me that Shandi was sleeping with his younger sister laughed, and I thought at first that incest was not considered to be so terrible. Then twelve-year-old Rombu came and asked if I had heard that Shandi was having sexual intercourse with his sister. I said I knew, and he said firmly, "I am very angry." I asked him why he should be angry, they were not Rombu's kin. He answered, "We are angry when someone sleeps with his sister." It was a strongly moral statement, and the word he used for sister was *poi.*

Considering Shandi's position in the social system, his affair with his sister is not completely astonishing. Shandi is about seventeen. The girls of his age are considered the most desirable women at Marcos. There is a word for girls in this nubile category, *shumboiya,* "having a water pot," a symbol for women's work, the age at which girls become women. Unmarried girls of this age take part in the work of the households. They are able to spin cotton and have started to learn to make hammocks. They spend a good part of their days dressing up, painting their faces, flirting and making love with men, married and unmarried, of twenty to forty years of age. They marry, often several times within the year, and none of them would consider an attachment to an ungainly adolescent. Marriage consists of a man moving his few possessions to the girl's house and tying his hammock and *mosquitero* next to hers. When marriages break up or, as the Sharanahua say, one "throws away" one's spouse, the man unties his hammock, takes his possessions, and leaves. The prepubescent girls, many of whom are already married, flirt and giggle but are already experts at evasion and teasing, aiming their wiles mostly again at men.

The young girls, six to ten, married or not, play house with the boys in what is called *faku-faku,* "child-child," an area hidden out behind the manioc gardens from adult view, where boys build small houses and bring a small bird or lizard for the girls to cook. Some sex play goes on, but a real attempt at sexual intercourse is reported to the adults. The girls are incessant tale bearers, reporting on each other as well as on the boys.

Although contact with Peruvians has added to the problems of adolescent boys, who now must win girls with trade goods as well as their hunting prowess, the period from about fifteen to twenty for boys would have been always a period of sexual deprivation. Years when learning to be a good hunter, to be a man and impress the provocative young women and their fathers, competing against full-grown men of longer experience, might make the younger sister who tags along beside you a tempting alternative. Shandi seems unable to make the Sharanahua transformation of tenderness to teasing, affection to antagonism, *poi* to *bimbiki.* His personal difficulty further empowers and validates the myth by demonstrating to boys like Rombu the temptation and condemnation of incest with *poi.* The structure of social roles is bolstered up, strengthened, and the play of daily life goes on.

The story of Moon and the other myths that I have heard were told, at my request, in the early evening at Basta's or Baiyakondi's house. At either house the circle of children whispering and giggling, the adults sitting on the raised floor or swaying in a hammock, were different, but everyone knew the myths. Everyone anticipated particularly good lines and imitated Basta's sound effects. Their interest was clear and this interest is held by the dilemma, the social tensions, that underlie myth as well as the well-dramatized presentation. The dilemma of Sharanahua men and those of other kinship organized societies is that *bimbiki* is desirable, but must be won in a competition with all one's brothers, while *poi* is available yet forbidden. In every society rules are broken as personal tensions generated by the structure itself conflict with the ideal morality.

There are no authority laden myths told at Marcos, no stories of strife between the generations or concern over incest between mother and son. As the myth seems to demonstrate, sister is essential since without her there can be no incest rule to break, and only through forbidding incest and exiling Moon can society continue. Moon's exile and subsequent sexual intercourse with the women of the *maloca* transforms girls into women with the onset of menstruation, which suggests the continuity of life through the ability to conceive. The myth of Moon is the Sharanahua rationalization of their conception of the social universe. An anthropologist's words are less vivid but, looking for the structure that orders the flux and flow of daily life, he too finds the crux of the social blueprint in the necessity of giving up one's own sister to gain another man's.

The structure that orders social relations within the village or within the old *malocas* is an exchange of sisters between men. One gives up *poi* to gain *bimbiki*, a sibling of the opposite sex for a cousin of the opposite sex. As a means of ordering the world of social relationships this is a simple and flexible model which makes it possible to produce or reproduce Sharanahua society with only a single brother and sister, as long as they find a brother and sister of another group who know the same rules. It is not surprising that some version of this social model is present in almost every tropical forest society that has been studied. Among many such groups men actually trade sister for sister; among the Sharanahua and others, men and women often actually marry their *bimbiki*, and whether or not their actual *poi* is given in exchange this is a structural principle underlying the categories of kinship.

The structure underlying the kinship system is that of two descent groups between whom marriages take place: the women of one group marrying the men of the other. It seems very likely that names such as Sharanahua, Chosinahua, and Marinahua have at times been merely the names of such descent groups between whom marriages take place. When these groups become large enough, however, the preference for marriage within the *maloca* leads to marriages of Sharanahua to Sharanahua, and the name comes to describe more than a single descent group, within which *unwu yura* are members of one's own descent group, close kinsmen who are not marriageable.

The boundaries of these descent groups are maintained by a rule of patrilineal descent. One is a Sharanahua because one's father was, so that Iconahua's children are Sharanahua though their mother is a Culina, and Tsatsa's children are Mastinahua like their father, though Tsatsa is a Sharanahua. Children are in the same group as their fathers, fathers' brothers and fathers' sisters. For a Sharanahua girl it was her father's sister who tatooed the permanent blue line on her face, the line that identifies her as a Sharanahua.

The structure of Sharanahua society assumes that children are in their father's descent group and, like their father, will marry someone in their mother's descent group. The incest taboo prohibits the possibility that these be the same descent group. If all the women of mother's descent group marry men in father's, the category of siblings includes the children of all fathers and all mothers. In contrast, since all father's sisters must marry into the other descent group, that is, must marry mother's brothers, their children will be in the other descent group, cousins who inherit their membership patrilineally through a mother's brother who is *their* father. Thus, all mother's brothers and father's sisters are potential fathers-in-law and mothers-in-law; all cousins of the opposite sex are potential spouses.

Personal names also tend to descend patrilineally, and Sharanahua usually name a child after its father's father or father's father's brothers or sisters. The alternation of generation which shows up in the kinship terms is reiterated by these names. Upon learning the name of a stranger one may instantly know whether to address him as "brother," "father," "mother's brother," or "cousin," and interact in the appropriate way.

Each category of kinship is bounded by three criteria: generation, sex, and descent group, and an ethnographer can predict the use of this system by any Sharanahua. Within this ordered pattern one is of my generation or the other, my sex or the other, my descent group or the other. The crucial contrast of the structure is that which distinguishes my generation, other sex, my descent group (*poi*) from my generation, other sex, other descent group (*bimbiki*). In a small society, sex and generation distinctions are perhaps obvious, born out in the responsibilities of daily activities, but the line between the descent groups is less obviously marked and must be underlined by the repetition of myth.

There are additions and changes to the basic structure. The terms *poi* and *futsa* have given way in usual conversations to the terms that emphasize relative age. Terms for grandparents are used interchangeably with the same generation terms, so that one may call mother's father, *chata* or *chai* (cousin of same sex); mother's mother, *chichi* or *chipi* (older sister), father's father, *shota* or *ochi* (older brother); father's mother, *shano* or *bimbiki* (cousin of opposite sex). Occasionally there is a further reversal, so that I have heard Yawandi trying to wheedle a bottle of perfume from her distant brother, Birata, say, "*shota* [father's father] give it to me." When referring to a grandparent, that is, saying, "Zacharais is my grandfather," Sharanahua always use the grandparent term rather than the same generation term. The same is true for children, nephews, and nieces. In speaking to a child the other generation terms are used, in referring to one's child, the term *faku* is used, including, of course brother's children for a male, sister's children for a female. Men refer to their sister's children as *unwu pia,* "my niece or nephew," women refer to their brother's children as *unwu rari,* "my niece or nephew."

Nowadays, children are born in their mother's parents' house so that they tend to be closer to their mother's parents, than they are to their father's parents. This may not have been true in the past when both sets of grandparents lived in the same *maloca.* Whenever I was asked about my own kinship group, the first grandparent mentioned was always *chata,* "mother's father."

A further elaboration of the basic structure is to use terms for affinals, people to whom one is related through marriage. The basic structure can be viewed as setting up categories of people, potential spouses, brothers-in-law, sisters-in-law, and parents-in-law. The actuality of marriage sets up specific relationships each of which is distinguished by a specific term. Thus, there is a term that is used to refer to "my wife," *unwu awi,* or "my husband," *unwu funi.* These are specific people, but the relationship is part of the general category of *bimbiki.*

Even with the additions and elaborations, one may discern a simple social script in which all the crucial roles are cast at birth, but in actuality the players often improvise, scheme, and manipulate their parts. In everyday life today and assuredly in the past, the social rules are modified or adjusted to meet shifting circumstances. Husbands and wives call each other *bimbiki* even though they have no such relationship before marriage. Additional relatives are sometimes added by calling any man *upa,* who "helped" conceive a child by making love to its mother during pregnancy. At times, distant relationships become hazy, so that people define them as it suits their needs. A family rich in kinsmen and wishing to discourage additional obligations may ignore a tenuous sibling relationship which stretches back to a father's father's brother's son's son, shrugging and saying in response to my questions, "He's nothing to me," or *"yura futsa."* At times a family with the same relationship but poor in kinsmen who might give them a share of game, will claim this "brother" as one of their own.

Ten-year-old Shomoni walked by my house one day, and I asked him where he was going. He told me he was going to visit his sister, Shomoiya. I sat, puzzling for a while since I had figured out that Shomoiya was properly his mother, even though she is only five years old. Taofaka walked by and asked me what I was doing, and I explained to him. He thought for a while and agreed that Shomoni was wrong. Shomoni may be wrong, but kinship roles are manipulatable, and he may have experienced the conflict between age and generation as untenable.

There are limits to the Sharanahua's use of their own system. The ethnographer can predict by his analysis of the system what one should call anyone, however distant the relationship, but Sharanahua tend to impose practical bounds on the distance to which they trace relationships. When I asked people what one called the children of a *chai,* "cousin of the same sex," some answered, "also *chai,*" most shrugged their shoulders and said, *"yura futsa"* or *"yamba fama,"* "my nothing."

The recent extreme disorganization of Sharanahua life, the loss of over half the population through epidemics shook the social structure and left cracks that time may patch over. The stories of those times came up when I questioned people on genealogies and marriages. The first time I asked Samuel what kinship term he had used for Ifama, before he took her as his wife, he did not hear me. I kept asking, and he finally answered, *"chiko,"* "a distant younger sister." She was just past puberty, her own parents, her brothers and sisters, had died in the measles epidemic, and her mother's sister had taken her in, but had treated her harshly. Her mother's brother asked Samuel if he wanted a wife. Samuel gave him a shirt and trousers purchased from the trader for whom he was working cedar. Ifama, having no father, came to live with Samuel in his father's house. Samuel was good, she says, and she had been alone. She holds onto Samuel and will not permit him to take another wife, although she knows that among his many mistresses is Yawandi, who has born him three children and has left her own husband several years ago. Ifama works harder than any woman at Marcos, yet she will not tolerate the idea of a second wife.

Ndaishiwaka also married a "sister," again in our terminology a distant cousin. Chatafundia, then about fourteen years old, had come to live with Shumundo, Ndaishiwaka's older sister. She slept in Shumundo's *mosquitero*, on the floor under her older sister's hammock. Ndaishiwaka wanted her but she refused to live with him for a year. Finally she accepted and, being like Ifama an orphan, came to live in Ndaishiwaka's house. A remarkably competent woman, Chatafundia has raised six children, nurses her own one year old and at times her youngest grandchild. Unlike Ifama, she is not a jealous wife, and she works well and cooperatively with Fando, her young co-wife. ("Fando" is a common Sharanahua name. This woman is not actually related to Zacharais, but she also called me "older sister.")

The two men's situations are superficially different in that Samuel was offered a girl for whom he had at first no particular desire, yet accepted, whereas Ndaishiwaka actively sought to take Chatafundia as his wife. The difference is not in the situation but in the extremely different personalities of the two men. These marriages would not have taken place if Sharanahua society had not been disorganized, the *maloca* gone, the population decimated. Even fifteen years after his marriage Samuel does not like to admit that Ifama is his "sister." Both men avoided working for and living with fathers-in-law by marrying girls who had no fathers, but girls whose kinship category put them outside the normal range of potential wives. In a period of less disorganization, Samuel would not have been offered Ifama as a wife, nor would Ndaishiwaka have desired Chatafundia.

Raiding used to provide an additional source of wives,

without the problems of dealing with a father-in-law. The continuous raiding and warfare of the past appear to have been the reason for the construction of the *maloca's* walls. They provided protection, which is no longer necessary. The Sharanahua say, "We are civilized," and are scornful of *indios bravos,* "wild Indians," despite their own recent history of warfare.

The pattern of the *maloca* continues, and men compete for their *bimbiki.* Warfare no longer exists, but young men still prefer to marry within their own villages, to have *koka* and *achi* as parents-in-law and to live near their kinsmen. There may be no girl available, however, and young men, like Moon, are forced out of their parents' houses or village to enter the household of *yura futsa.*

EXTENDED HOUSEHOLDS

The Organization of Security

The layout of Marcos today, the social ties that determine where each house is built, how close it is to its·neighbor, how open to view, is partially based on a blueprint that derives from the *malocas* of 1925 built on the small streams of the river Yaminahua, an affluent of the Embira River. In 1925, the three most important men at Marcos, Baiyakondi, Zacharais, and Basta, were young men, living in a *maloca* with numerous other Sharanahua on the Yaminahua River. Baiyakondi, the eldest of the three, was married to Basta's sister. Zacharais' older sister was Basta's father's second wife. These ties have been transformed through the years so that now the marriages that tie these men and their descendants together are those between Basta and Zacharais' two daughters, Basta's son and Baiyakondi's granddaughter, Zacharais' daughter and Baiyakondi's son.

Kinship and marriage still tie each household into the village, but walls no longer contain them in total proximity. The layout of the village itself is an on-the-ground diagram of relationships in which physical distance coincides with social distance, physical proximity to close social ties. It is a five minute's walk from Baiyakondi's house to Zacharais', and the path meanders through heavy brush which completely blocks the view, until one reaches the clearing and Zacharais' large house. The ground is cleared between his and his son-in-law's, Basta's, house, and sitting in Zacharais' house, one can watch the women at Basta's preparing a meal.

The Sharanahua bring their past to Marcos in the expectations and obligations of sets of social relationships, learned in childhood, conflicting and adjusting to the realities of each day. The crucial reality of Sharanahua life is the necessity for insuring a secure food supply and this fact shapes the interactions between men and women, old and young, kinsmen and affinals.

No two days are alike at Marcos, but no two days are really different. Tasks vary only slightly from day to day, from dry season to rainy season, from times when there are hundreds of turtle eggs to times when small children, full of milk and plantains and manioc, scream at their mothers for meat. Food is abundant, yet obtaining food is a never-ending quest. Occasionally there may be more meat or fish than the entire village can eat in one day so that at each cookhouse meat is slowly roasting to keep it for three days. But then there will be nothing, and men must take their chances on hunting. The Sharanahua cannot plan their days or weeks or years knowing that food is taken care of so that they can, therefore, concentrate on some other enterprise.

Women go through their daily rounds, starting the cook fire, fetching water in large trade pots during their early morning bath before the mist has been burned off the river by the sun. Bathing early when the river feels warm but the chill air still bites is considered a proper act, a virtue that distinguishes the Sharanahua from their dirty neighbors. On the days when my Sharanahua mood is strong, I have gone also with a kettle for water, with five-year-old Shomoiya as chaperon. Both Shomoiya and I dread the chill, and splash ourselves briefly and are rewarded by being greeted on our return with social approval and the smugness of virtue as we ask others if they have bathed yet.

The men bathe as the women cook *mania butsa,* "plantain drink," returning to take bowlfuls of the hot, sweet drink. While the women heat fish or meat and yesterday's manioc for breakfast, men casually visit at other households, taking more *mania butsa* and quietly making plans for hunting or fishing, working on canoes, and estimating who else will be hunting today.

Onsika leaves early to hunt. He is the best hunter at Marcos, and many men wish to accompany him since if two men hunt together they will split the game. Onsika is an Amahuaca, *yura futsa,* living in his father-in-law's house, married to a shrew with five children who clamor for meat. A few men take canoes and hunt together; others walk into the forest by the trails that start behind each house.

In each household one wife or daughter stays with the small children or carries one in a woven sling, while one woman or more goes to harvest manioc, or canoe loads of women leave for upriver banana gardens. Mornings are the quietest times in the village, a few men repairing their guns or bows and arrows, a few women and girls tending small children, until the sun reaches the height of midday, and women return from their gardens with heavy baskets pulling the tumpline of fiber tight across their foreheads.

Everyone bathes saying, "I'm sweaty," before another meal is prepared. A huge pot of manioc is set to steam, enough for an entire day. Women from other households casually drop by, there may be no meat or fish left in their houses. I usually plan my day so as to be at Basta's house. Sometimes I offer canned tuna fish or sardines, the small cans rapidly vanishing in the large household, so that no one has quite enough to feel satisfied. Rombu shares a piece with his younger sister who tries to keep it despite the irate demands of Comafo, her brother's son. But her mother insists, "You're selfish, give it to your *upa.*"

The men start to return, beaching their canoes and walking up from the river to their houses or walking the household's trail from the forest. Although at Basta's house, Yawandi peers

Fando, Ndaishiwaka's younger wife, preparing food in the cookhouse
The younger girl is her daughter; the older is Chatafundia's

through the cracks in the wall when a man walks by, she rarely
sees a man returning with game to any house but her own and
Zacharais'. A large animal is carried on a man's back secured
by fiber straps; a small animal is carried in a makeshift basket
of green thatch. Peccary and deer skins are saleable, and a man
very carefully places one on banana leaves and skins it as a
few children hold its feet. The skin is then staked down with
slivers of bamboo onto a soft wooden board to dry in the sun.

The actual butchering of all game is done by the oldest
wife of the household owner. If the skin is not valuable she
takes over immediately, sometimes giving another woman the
chore of dipping the animal into boiling water and pulling off

Birata, Samuel's son-in-law, skinning one of the two peccaries he has shot

Boy eating the peccary's testicles which his *koka*, Birata, gave him while Samuel skinned the second peccary

its fur. Any large animal is divided into four quarters, leaving the head and back as a fifth piece. The butchering is done rapidly and skillfully. The meat is protected from dirt by a layer of banana leaves, the contents of the body cavity are removed with a minimum of blood spilled. The liver and heart are kept, sometimes the intestines are washed out to cook, and the rest is thrown at a distance from the house where the ducks and dogs compete for a piece. If one of the emaciated dogs sniffs too closely while the meat is being cut, he is hit hard with a stick or the back of a machete and limps away, yelping with pain.

At Basta's house Naikashu gives half a peccary to her mother, Yawanini, and sends a girl to call Chatafundia to come and take a quarter. The organization is swift and efficient. Sometimes Naikashu gestures to Tarani to bring Basta his food and banana drink, and Yawandi has the fire going hot under a pot filled with water as the meat is cut into fist-size portions and dropped in, and within half an hour from the time Naikashu started her work the meat is out of sight cooking. The women exclaim over any fat in the animal and roast it wrapped in leaves with the liver and intestines and dip their fingers or a piece of manioc into the liquid grease and eat it avidly.

The men have bathed on their return, the women bathe again while the meat cooks, and the members of the household sit in their hammocks, Basta sitting somewhat apart in the cookhouse, yet commenting on the silly laughter of women. His young son-in-law sits on the steps on the other side of the house. Naikashu sews her daughter's dress, Bashkondi spins cotton, Yawandi tells me some gossip. Visiting goes on by sex and age and kin group, so that old Baido may come and sit with Basta; Samuel leans against the high floor and talks to Bashkondi, his sister, while Shomoiya, his daughter, plays with dolls with her cousin, Basta's youngest daughter.

When the meat is cooked, Naikashu dishes out a number of plates, signaling to Yawandi and Bashkondi to serve. She allots the best pieces to Basta, who may ask Baido or his youngest two sons to join him. Two of the recently married young women take plates of meat and manioc to eat with their husbands. Naikashu, Yawandi, and Bashkondi share their plates with me and call over their children. If there is a great deal of meat, Naikashu may send Tarani to call the women of a more distant house, and she will send a plate of meat to Baiyakondi.

The meal is served and, tearing pieces of meat off the shared chunks, sipping broth made doubly hot with strong pepper, taking bites of the carefully steamed manioc, the day appears replete with satisfaction. There is water to rinse off one's hands after a meal, and more water for the women to rinse off the enameled tin plates and gourd bowls.

Everyone bathes at least once again during the remaining hours of daylight, in part because perspiration intensifies the incessant attack of gnats, in part because perspiration is unsightly and uncomfortable. The women paint their own faces and their children's, work on cotton or bead necklaces, men swing in their hammocks, repair a fish net, or play with their smallest child. Another meal may be served before nightfall or, if visitors are not wanted, after dark, when most people are in their houses and glints of kerosene lamps or rubber torches break the darkness.

The easy and smooth-flowing organization of daily chores at Marcos is based on the division of labor and the assignment of specific tasks within each extended family household. Economic roles are assigned by sex, and the division of labor is strict at Marcos. It is unthinkable for a man to harvest or carry manioc; it is laughable to conceive of a woman with a bow and arrow in her hand. The gluing of economic roles to the basic sex roles leads to the unescapable fact that if a woman would eat meat, she must have a relationship with a hunter; a man who desires wild palm fruits and cooked foods must associate with a woman. The organization of subsistence, therefore, involves relating the sexes in permanent or temporary association to carry out work and to share its products.

The women of Basta's household washing clothes

The minimum number of people necessary to maintain a viable household at Marcos are two adult men and two adult women, with the older man somewhat more responsible than the younger; the older woman tending to direct the tasks of other women of the household. In the history of any household this complement is maintained, but the membership changes over time. To arbitrarily take a starting point in the cycle, a young man marries a child and moves into his father-in-law's house. He is expected to hunt and fish and gather turtle eggs. His father-in-law usually has two wives for whom he hunts and clears gardens. The women cooperate in caring for their children, collecting wild foods, harvesting crops, and preparing food. As years pass the young wife becomes a woman, and children are born in their grandparents' house. The father-in-law clears gardens for his daughter as well as his wives, and the young son-in-law also begins to clear gardens for his wife. If one of the father-in-law's wives die, there are still two adult women in the household, and he will probably not take another wife. As the father-in-law grows older, he hunts less, but still clears gardens. The younger man will either take his wife's sister as a second wife or will try to win a girl with no father since he is unable to live simultaneously with two fathers-in-law. If he can then attract a son-in-law by marrying off his own daughter, he is in a position to start his own household. As long as his father-in-law lives, however, his wife's ties to her father and mother will link the two households together.

Samuel tried for a few months to maintain a household consisting only of his nuclear family. At the point that he first had a son-in-law, he had started to build a house set just out of sight of his father's large household. Birata, his son-in-law, married Ahuiyumba, who was then about twelve years old, still a child who had not yet reached puberty. Birata is a good hunter, and the household seemed viable as long as Birata stayed, although Ifama, Samuel's wife, worked harder than most women despite Ahuiyumba's assistance. Like many of the young men who take child brides, Birata did not stay long. He left Marcos for several months, and when he returned married another child, one of Ndaishiwaka's daughters. Samuel tried to maintain his own small household, but within a very short time he gave up and returned to Zacharais'.

A year later, when Tararai married Ahuiyumba, Samuel again moved away into his own house. This time he moved his old house over to the river bank, building another small one next to it for Ahuiyumba and Tararai. Despite the two dwellings there was only one cookhouse, and Ahuiyumba was still completely part of her parents' household. The small second dwelling was used mainly for sleeping, and often her two younger sisters joined Ahuiyumba and Tararai. In 1969 Samuel was building a large house to include his entire family. If Tararai remains with Ahuiyumba, Samuel may be successful in his effort to achieve a separate household. Only necessity drove him back to his father's where he has neither responsibilities nor advantages. Had he a father-in-law, he would probably have waited until Ahuiyumba was a woman and her marriage secure.

Girls of Ahuiyumba's age, just before puberty, are able assistants, but they are only beginning to learn the skills of basketry, spinning, and weaving. Meals are more varied and crafts, such as basket making and weaving, are more frequently undertaken with several women to share in the work. Two men and two women are the minimum number that can maintain an independent household, but households with more women to share the diverse tasks appear better off.

Yawandi told me a myth about a father who was angered by his baby daughter's crying and threw her out of his house.

A jaguar seized the baby daughter, and her father wept, believing that the jaguar had eaten her. The jaguar took care of her and married her when she became a woman. She gave birth to three jaguar babies. One day the jaguar went hunting, and the father came to the house. The woman cried and asked, "Father, why did you throw me out, now I am a jaguar's wife."

The jaguar returned from hunting with five peccaries in a tiny basket and started to growl at his wife's father. "Don't be angry," she said, "it's my father." They ate the meat and slept.

In the morning the father started to leave and said, "I'm going, daughter." The jaguar was angry and threatening, but the father blew on his hands, and the jaguar died. Father and daughter went to the father's house where the woman took a new husband, her jaguar children died, and she bore a human child.

The myth seems to suggest that a woman who marries outside of her father's house lives with a dangerous stranger. A Sharanahua who throws away a daughter cannot gain a son-in-law. Only by holding onto their daughters can men insure that there will be a way of luring a son-in-law to the house. Young women may be contemptuous of teen-age boys, but their fathers woo likely young men such as Dikandi, an Amahuaca boy about fifteen years old, the finest procurer of turtles, turtle eggs, small game, and fish at Marcos.

A young man usually has no role in his parents' household. As a boy, his father may invite him to share his plate of food occasionally, but as he matures he is more of a burden than an asset. A girl regards her father's house as an almost permanent home in which she has rights and obligations, in which she is an important productive member as soon as she is able to carry out women's skills. A boy, however, begins to roam with his brothers and cousins, hunting birds and frogs, cadging meals at the households of his other fathers or mothers' brothers, rarely hunting with or helping his father. Women and girls spend their days together. Little girls and grown daughters eat within the household, while their older brothers are called to eat only in the evening.

The daughters of a household flirt with and tease their older sister's husband. They bring him food, they help to mend his clothes and weave his hammock, they may well become his other wives some day. Their brother receives none of these attentions. He must find a willing girl or a willing father-in-law. If he is lucky one of his *bimbiki* is unmarried and he can move into the household of his mother's brother or father's sister, kinsmen he has known all his life. However, there is a shortage of young women at Marcos, even though there are more adult women than men. Polygyny takes young women out of the available category, and only mature men are able to gain two wives. This, of course, leaves fewer women available, and young men are often forced out of their own village to live with a foreign set of in-laws and to marry girls below the age of puberty, girls with whom they may not have sexual intercourse.

This prohibition appears to be respected, although it is impossible to be sure. Birata, a young man of about twenty-two was married for a while to Ahuiyumba, then about twelve years of age and not yet menstruating.* Birata had come to my house to have his foot treated, and Ahuiyumba was sitting, talking to him while he soaked his foot. He was fairly drunk that afternoon and put his arm around Ahuiyumba, pulling her toward him. She was a small girl, but she hit him as hard as she could. He instantly dropped his arm and moved away, certainly not out of fear, but somewhat guiltily.

He must wait until his wife has her first menstrual flow before consummating the marriage. Since this may be years away, young men often leave the household or even the village unless they are able to find willing lovers within the village. Sharanahua have learned to make rings from Peruvian coins, and young men often give such rings to their mistresses, and some girls collect two or three at a time.

Mature men, however, have the advantage at Marcos. In gaining mistresses and in keeping wives the men of thirty and forty are most often the winners. Thus, Tararai lost his first wife, Ipo, to Iconahua. She was about nineteen, flirtatious and provocative, and Iconahua, a man of thirty-five with one wife already, apparently found it easy to lure her away. Several men told Tararai to act like a Peruvian and defend his honor, so Tararai gave Ipo a vicious swipe with a machete, inflicting a gash on her head. She recovered and Iconahua and Ipo left Marcos for a few months, leaving Tomuha, the first wife behind. She grieved for her husband and said she would wait for him to return. The

*In modern urban societies the age of menarche is steadily dropping, but among people such as the Sharanahua, the average age at menarche is estimated at fifteen to seventeen.

household is a successful one. Tomuha and Ipo cooperate well and spend a great deal of time laughing and telling stories together despite a ten year age difference. Like most co-wives they take turns caring for the children and carrying out the gardening, gathering, and doing the multiple activities that fall to women. Tararai was, for a while, desolate, temporarily hung his hammock in the house of a distant sister and, a year later, married Ahuiyumba, still a child, who had by then "thrown out" her husband, Birata.

A young man arranges with his father-in-law to marry a girl of perhaps seven years of age. Little girls are sometimes affectionate to their husbands, but they usually ignore them until they are closer to adolescence at fourteen or fifteen. If you ask them about their husbands, they giggle and go on playing with their sisters and cousins. The important relationship is between the son-in-law and his parents-in-law, who call each other *raisi*. One day I was trying to remember the name of one young man. I asked several people by referring to him as "Ruatay's husband." Everyone looked puzzled and since there was more than one girl named Ruatay in the village I clarified the question by specifying that she was Basharua's daughter. Someone laughed then at the phrase, "Ruatay's husband," and said, "You mean Bito, Basharua's *raisi*." Whereas the basic kinship terms distinguish categories of people, *raisi* describes a specific and unique relationship. The term is reciprocal between son-in-law and parents-in-law, and it is used as well by all the siblings of the parents-in-law. It can be translated as a relationship between two members of different generations affinally related (that is, related by marriage) through a woman.

The young man gains a house to live in and a mother-in-law and other adult women who will prepare food for him and provide him with all the economic services that are women's domain. The household gains a hunter and a future clearer of gardens. *Raisi* is often a foreigner, *yura futsa,* and is treated with distance by his in-laws. He eats apart with his wife and her younger sisters, sometimes finds another young man in a similar position, and often spends a great deal of time lying idly in his hammock, bored and, perhaps, lonely.

The Sharanahua extended household depends upon the strength of the matrilocal rule, that men must live in their father-in-law's house. This is a rule not simply of social checkers, but a rule with strong emotional affect. Two years ago when Koyo was about sixteen she married Tolivio's son. This was her third marriage of that year and she agreed, although unhappily, that she would go for a while to stay at Tolivio's village, Canto Gallo, eight-hours downstream. Tolivio was at this time making *fariña*, roasted manioc flour, to sell to a Peruvian, and he insisted that he needed his son's assistance.

I passed Canto Gallo a month or so later on a trip downriver, and we stopped to beg for bananas. Koyo came running and bitterly complained to me about the terrible people in this village. They were angry and selfish, and she missed Marcos. She tried to run away a few weeks later, but Tolivio and her husband brought her back. Then word came upriver to Marcos that Koyo was pregnant. The women of Basta's house went downriver by canoe to bring her back, and for several months they lived in Basta's house. Koyo never had a baby, she had made the one sure move that would enforce her return since a baby must be born in the house of its mother's father. Koyo eventually threw her husband away and married an older and more sophisticated man and lived at Basta's. When I was last at Marcos in 1969, Koyo was truly pregnant, and this marriage appeared to be lasting.

The father-in-law makes the decision about his son-in-law while his daughter is very young, but the adolescent girls usually have more to say and often choose their own husbands. I lived for two months in the same house as Tararai and Ahuiyumba and, after an almost sleepless night due to Tararai's drunken singing, asked Samuel rather strongly why he had ever wanted Tararai as his *raisi*. Samuel replied that he had not particularly wanted Tararai at all, but Ahuiyumba, close to puberty, had wept and screamed and bothered him until he agreed to her marriage. In contrast, Bashkondi told me that she had never wanted to marry Basta, but that when she was still a child her father had beaten her into following her older sister and becoming Basta's second wife.

The extended, matrilocal family is the basic building block of the Sharanahua today. Samuel, Shamarua, and Iconahua have avoided matrilocality by marrying orphans, but the only true exception to the matrilocal rule is Gustavo, who lives in his father's house even though his wife's father is alive. Gustavo fulfills many of the obligations of a son-in-law. He has made a dug-out canoe for Ndaishiwaka, his father-in-law, and has started to clear gardens for Ishamba, his wife. I suspect that Ndaishiwaka and Ndaishiwaka's wife find it more useful to have an important connection with Basta's household than to directly add another son-in-law, a hunter, to their own household. As the myth of the jaguar indicates, a son-in-law's importance is his contribution as a hunter. Ndaishiwaka has one son-in-law already living in the household. The addition of another would be difficult since two young men might compete for the same woman within the house, and if Gustavo moved in he would have reason to expect that Ishamba's younger sisters should be his other wives when they reach twelve or thirteen. The marriage between Gustavo and Ishamba provides Ndaishiwaka's household with an important link to Basta's household. This connection permits Ndaishiwaka's household to receive meat from Basta's, and Basta's household both receives and gives a good deal of meat.

In reply to the question, "To whom do you give meat?" the Sharanahua say, "We give it to everyone." But if one observes the actual distribution of meat, one finds that it is shared with specific kin. The distribution is always carried out by women in Naikashu's position, the first wife of the owner of the household (when she is ill or temporarily away, Yawandi, Basta's daughter, takes over). It makes no difference whether the game has been killed by Naikashu's husband, her son-in-law, or her son, the distribution follows the same pattern: A large share goes first to her mother, while smaller shares, if there is enough, go to her siblings. As long as a woman's parents are alive they will receive meat from the household of their son-in-law. In contrast, as with Ndaishiwaka, a man may live next to his father's house with no obligation to bring him meat, once he is no longer a member of his father's household.

Naikashu frequently gives a quarter of a peccary to Ndaishiwaka's house. According to Ndaishiwaka this is because Naikashu is his sister, the daughter of his father's brother. Ndaishiwaka's brother, Iconahua, however, never receives meat from this source, and he stands in exactly the same relationship. The difference between them is that Ndaishiwaka's daughter, Ishamba, is married to Basta's son, and the couple live in Basta's house. Ishamba spends a great deal of time in her father's house, and Chatafundia is a reliable mother, who properly sends a plate of food to Ishamba every day. In addition, Chatafundia often sends meat to Naikashu, even when it is but a small monkey, and she is particularly adept at appearing at Naikashu's house with a bowl of plantains just as Naikashu is cutting up game. At Marcos, one gives in order to receive, and one is trapped by kinsmen bearing food.

Recently Shirimba, a woman known for her stinginess, started to appear at Basta's house each day, carrying a plate of food to Basta's new son-in-law. Puzzled, I asked Yawandi what was happening since I knew Shirimba's reputation. Yawandi and several other women laughed and said he was her "younger brother," although very distantly, and we all smiled knowingly at Shirimba's attempt to set up a tie with Basta's household. In particular, a tie that would permit her to expect a quarter of an animal in exchange for a cooked portion of food. Although Shirimba's husband hunts often and well, he is providing for a large household. His father-in-law, Baido, is an old man, who gardens actively but hunts little. The other man in the household, Shirimba's brother, hunts only a few days during the month. Shirimba has five children. Baido has only one kinsman in the world, Zacharais, his mother's brother, and Shirimba's husband, an Amahuaca, has none. No one has ever excused Shirimba's stinginess on the grounds that she is seldom in a position to give meat away and has no kin from whom she can regularly expect to receive it.

Kinsmen provide security, and if one is adept at reciprocity like Chatafundia one can count fairly well on a steady diet of meat. In contrast, Samuel and Ifama are poor at the distribution game. Samuel is a poor hunter, and Tararai is a typically lazy son-in-law. Yet even when there is a good catch of fish, Ifama is tempted to keep it all rather than sweeten her kinship links with a judicious gift. Samuel's mother, Yawanini, came sternly over to the house one afternoon to demand a large fish. While it is true that a son need give nothing to his mother or father, Yawanini or Naikashu at Basta's house might be encouraged to share food more often if Ifama made significant offers.

The key to the distribution system is reciprocity. It is not enough to be a kinsman; nonkin are simply out of the game, and the divisions of kinship or affinal relationship provide the ground rules. No household will continue to distribute meat to a household that does not reciprocate. Between households such as Basta's and Zacharais', where Basta is married to two of Zacharais' daughters, reciprocity is continual. Only animals such as birds, small turtles, or small monkeys are not shared. But as one moves beyond this clear-cut affinal link, there are a number of crosscutting kinship ties, anyone of which is a possible obligation. This is due in part to the overlapping and unclear kinship relationships that have resulted from the loss of population through epidemics during the past twenty-five years, and the inclusion of foreigners and distant relatives within the village. The increasing importance of the affinal tie between households seems to be a partial solution to the problem of defining and limiting kinship obligations.

A Sharanahua still cannot refuse a request for food from kin, but the overlapping of many distant kinship ties makes it more difficult today for anyone to be sure that a kinsman to whom he gives game will include him in his distribution. Women are continually complaining that they give meat away, but it is not reciprocated. Giving and reciprocation are constant only with the one other linked household. Where there is no affinal tie, one or more kinship links are usually selected for continuous reciprocity, but the return is seldom as sure. Stressing the affinal tie gives some assurance that reciprocation will follow a gift of meat.

The bulk of the diet at Marcos consists approximately of 60 per cent agricultural produce, 30 per cent game, 5 per cent fish, and 5 per cent gathered food. Meat is relatively abundant at Marcos, and it is rare for more than three or four days to go by without meat in a house. The Sharanahua are continually preoccupied with the topic of meat, and men, women, and children spend an inordinate amount of time talking about meat, planning visits to households that have meat, and lying about the meat they have in their own households.

The Sharanahua value generosity and, after a successful hunt, most people clearly enjoy sending off invitations to eat. These invitations are rarely extended to an entire household and seldom to an entire family. Men invite their brothers or cousins of the same sex; women invite their sisters and female cousins. On a day that meat is plentiful, people go from house to house eating at each one. When meat is scarce, invitations are not forthcoming, and a great deal of apparently casual visiting takes place. This visiting is also done separately by various members of the household. A man will drop in at his brother's house and sit for a while until a meal is served. Women with their younger children visit their sisters. Older children travel their own routes, stopping at the house of their other "mothers" or "fathers," mother's brothers or father's sisters.

This develops into a social waiting game in which the guests make conversation and the hosts put off eating. The only mention of food is the sorrowful *"nami yamai,"* "there is no more meat." Lying is an essential social grace at Marcos, while a direct refusal is insulting. Sooner or later the guests give up or the host takes out the food and says, *"no pino,"* "let's eat." A close relative is always fed if he is present during the time that a meal is served. A distant relative who appears at mealtime may not be invited to sit or eat, but stays on the outskirts of the group who are eating, reaching for a piece of manioc and meat from time to time. Nonkin will not attempt to eat in the absence of an invitation, and they may be totally ignored.

When there is only a small amount of meat in the house, when one small wild bird must stretch for a household of ten, or a few chunks of meat remain from the day before, carefully stored out of sight in a basket hanging from the rafters, the obligation to feed one's kin is a burden. One shakes one's head sorrowfully and says, *"nami yamai."*

Lying and secrecy solve a conflict between widespread kinship obligations and a small amount of game. When a great deal of meat is brought into the village, the ideal of giving to all one's kin can be met. It is exceedingly difficult for a Sharanahua to refuse to share food when confronted by a member of his kinship group. Secrecy helps to limit the confrontation. A Peruvian who hunts the same animals in the same way is not secretive about meat. He has no obligation to share it with a meatless neighbor. The Sharanahua, on the other hand, feel obliged to share with all kin. Secrecy is the mode of adapting to this pressure, while the same set of values is maintained.

In the *maloca,* hunting was probably more often a collective effort before shotguns and shells began to replace bows and arrows. Collective hunting, occasionally occurring today in the special hunt, brought in a larger amount of meat at one time, and the ideal of sharing meat within the entire *maloca* could be met.

While the communal *maloca* probably enforced the rule that meat should be shared, today's settlement pattern appears specifically designed to make secrecy possible, except with one closely linked household, which is clearly in view. The household trails to port and forest make it difficult to know if someone is or is not returning to his house with meat. The solitary hunter, returning from the forest, walks his private path and hands over his game to the women of the household in the cookhouse behind the house.

When meat is distributed women send children to call women of other households to come for their share. When anyone is heard or seen going past a house, some of the women try to find out who may be bringing or receiving meat. They ask the children where they are going. Occasionally they are answered, but usually the reply is a vague, "Over there."

Besides these physical measures providing secrecy about hunting, cultural norms additionally inhibit access to information about the meat supply, It is considered rude or inappropriate either to brag about one's own success in the hunt or to enquire about someone else's. Should the question indirectly be raised, the usual answer is "There is no more meat," or "I have no shells," even though the pot may be full and several shells are concealed in one's house. I was the only one who ever asked directly whether or not someone had brought back game. This restriction means that even when the physical restrictions to information gathering are overcome—and children particularly often manage to gain such information—it cannot be acted upon.

During the month that I was gathering a day by day record of hunting and the distribution of meat, it quickly became clear that on this topic my informants were seldom well informed and rarely trustworthy and that only actual observations would yield these data. Even when I spent the full day trying to track down such information, I was unable to include the entire village in my survey. After limiting the attempt to three households, I found it necessary to refuse all offers of meat or invitations from these households in order to collect accurate data.

A further hazard was that once people understood my objectives, they attempted to question me as to who had been hunting and who had received meat. On one occasion I slipped up and gave away this information to a woman who had not been called to a distribution of meat. I had encountered Tohukai, talking to Tomuha, his brother's wife. Knowing that Tohukai had been hunting that morning and eager to get the information for my hunting record, I asked if he had brought back any game. After an awkward silence, Tohukai acknowledged that he had brought back a peccary. A few minutes later when I went to his house to watch Yawanini, his mother-in-law, distribute the peccary, Tomuha also appeared and was given a piece of the back. Tomuha rarely received meat from this household and never gave meat to them, so that her presence there was clearly due to the information she had received through my blunder. Apparently it was possible for Tomuha to act on information received from an outsider, while it would not have been possible for her to act if Tohukai himself had told her, which clearly he had not done. It seems more than coincidental that the day following my slip, I was told by the women of Yawanini's house that Tomuha had been stealing from me. I was friendly with Tomuha and even if it were true, there was no apparent reason to tell me. It had the effect, however, of temporarily putting a strain on our relationship. Since all distribution of meat is carried out by women to women, the disapproval of other women is a strong sanction against making use of information even where secrecy fails.

From a Sharanahua's point of view, secrecy allows him to maintain his expectation of profiting from kinship obligations —the possibility of receiving meat while hoarding his shells.

From the ethnographer's point of view, secrecy maintains the distribution of meat by blinding the participants to the inequality of their efforts and their rewards.

Hunting is a chancy pursuit, and a village with many men, in which meat is shared, secures a steadier supply of meat to all and provides some insurance against the bad luck, illness, or lack of skill of a single hunter providing for a single family. The size of many animals further encourages sharing since a single family may not be able to consume the meat before it rots in the tropical climate.

At the moment, and this moment may have a fifty-year duration, the crosscutting interactions that provide the Sharanahua with a secure food supply have created the pattern of Marcos. The pattern is one of extended family households, each linked closely to one other household and loosely grouped in a village. Ties are strong within the extended household and with its closely linked neighbor, and, traveling the Upper Purús, one encounters such paired households that have broken with village ties completely and settled together. Village ties are weak, supported by loyalty to members of one's own descent group and identification with members of one's own sex.

The presence of a missionary at Marcos has, for the moment, increased stability, but the *maloca* is gone, and Sharanahua households are spread out within the village, still following the old social plan, but an expanded version. It is as if stress and tension had blown the communal house apart, spacing out extended families at a more comfortable distance.

VILLAGE

Hunting and Collecting,
The Battle of the Sexes

I have never gone hunting since no man at Marcos would tolerate a woman's presence in this context. Ndaishiwaka agreed several times to let me accompany him, but somehow he always left earlier than he had indicated or changed his mind at the last minute. What I know of hunting, therefore, is known only through my informants, who describe going into the forest along the hunting trails, looking for the track or spoor of an animal, and following it till it is in sight. I know that Sharanahua can identify the track of any animal where I see barely an indentation in the soil.

Men usually hunt with single barrel, breech-loading shotguns. Powder and shot are unknown in this area. Since shells are expensive, men try to reuse them by digging the pellets out of the game and repacking them in the plastic shell case. Every man at Marcos still keeps bow and arrows stored in the rafters in case he runs out of shells or breaks his gun.

Men search first for the traces of large animals: deer, tapir, peccary, capybara, paca; but as the sun climbs high they may settle for a wild bird, a monkey, or a land turtle. Armadillos are usually small, but they are desirable as the meat is sweet and considered a delicacy. Men may eat armadillos, and women who have born at least three children may share the meat. Other women will be made sterile if they partake. Jaguars and ocelots are never eaten by the Sharanahua, neither are foxes, ant-eaters, nor porcupines; they say they have learned to dislike porcupines from the Peruvians.

Sharanahua like to bring meat home, but the men are not enthusiastic about hunting. "We hunt," they say, "because our wives and children cry for meat." While I have never hunted, I have gone with a group of men and women to carry tapir meat back to Marcos. Sharafo had shot two tapirs with bow and arrows the day before. It was growing late, and the tapirs were far to heavy for him to carry alone. He covered them with palm thatch to protect them from scavengers and returned to Marcos announcing his catch. The next day about eight of us walked for two hours through the forest and found the tapirs, still untouched, the thick skin protecting the meat from insects but alive with the large ticks of the tapir. The men hacked the tapirs into carrying-size portions; the women fashioned carrying baskets of green thatch lined with leaves. Heavily burdened we brought the meat back to Marcos, each carrying his portion back to his own household. It was during the rainy season, and the path seemed endless, up over slippery mud and down through swamps, soaking us to the hips. The meat attracted flies, and we attracted ticks, so that returning from the forest we each had to carefully check to remove each tiny tick from our bodies. Hunting is best in the rainy season since animal tracks are more easily distinguished than in the hard dirt of the dry season.

Collecting in the forest with a bunch of women and children is usually a light-hearted expedition, only a short walk into the forest. Someone has been told of a tree filled with wild cherries, or ripening clusters of palm nuts or palm fruits. Several households of women set out at no particular time of day, whenever more serious chores are completed. We track through the forest, Shimiri or Tarani warning me which tree has thorns,

which ants will sting. The forest is cool even when the high sun
pounds on the village, and we walk across the log bridges crossing streams. Yawandi notes a particularly good tree for thatch.
Bashkondi offers me a few leaves which I, suspecting some trick,
refuse. It is a plant, she admits, that makes women conceive.
Small children jounce in their mother's or sister's carrying sling,
and a young dog, still eager, pushes by to reach the first in line.

A short way from Marcos the ground is uneven, and we
climb up and through and over the cut-down trees in Basta's
new garden, then back into the forest. We rarely encounter an
animal or a snake along the path, though women often stop
and listen, hearing a macaw in the high canopy above us or a
monkey far off, shouting warning. We arrive at our goal, and the
women place leaves in a shaded place for the small children to
sit upon. One or two older children entertain the little ones,
while the women work with their machetes cutting the branches
of fruits or berries, stripping them into the thatch carrying
baskets. The forest takes on a domestic quality as the small
children play or sleep; the women work, gossip, and laugh.
Sometimes the group splits up, some returning ahead of the
others. Once three of us were lost for a while, starting several
trails and going in circles with a touch of fright. Shimiri began
to make the sound of a bird, calling to the others through the
forest. Finally a high-pitched call responded and with laughter
directed our path. The Sharanahua are frightened in the forest
when the path is unclear, and they keep away from the forest
at night when spirits search for the flesh of men. Animals were
once humans, and at night perhaps the distinction is once more
blurred.

Yawandi told the following myth:

Everyone went to the forest. A beautiful woman, an older
woman like Naikashu, found some duck-like eggs. She took
them, cooked them, and gave all the women a little bit.
All the women ate the small pieces of egg and made corn

drink. The men went out hunting and when they returned carrying lots of meat, they found all the women were sleeping. The men saw the egg and wondered what it was. They smelled it and fell asleep.

Some small children began to cry, and then turned into peccaries. The women said, "How come my child has become a peccary?" and the women turned into peccaries. The men said, "My wife has turned into a peccary," and they turned into peccaries.

Two men were hiding in another *maloca*. They saw all the peccaries, but they didn't understand what had happened. The peccaries went off into the forest. The two men decided to go back to their house since all their people were now peccaries. They found the egg shell, smelled it, and went back to their house. A rotten branch fell on their house. The men yelled and turned into small peccaries.

All the peccaries were crying. An owl warned them that someone was coming, and all but one of the peccaries fled. A man killed it with an arrow. The other peccaries were angry and fled further into the forest. The owl warned them that people were coming. The men killed some of them, while the others fled to the sky. All the people-peccaries are in the sky. We eat their children which are on earth. Spirits eat the large ones in the sky.

This myth describes the origin of the two animals most frequently hunted by the Sharanahua, *yawa*, the large white-lipped peccary, and *ondo*, the smaller collared peccary. It seems to show how women, the collectors, transform men into hunters, by creating *yawa* and *ondo* through a reverse evolution in which animals descend from men. In one sense this evolutionary picture is accurate as it is the creation of hunting that produces game since an animal becomes game only when it is hunted. The corn drink in the myth further relates women's role to men's hunting since this is the drink that a woman gives to the man who hunts for her in the Sharanahua special hunt.

Women in their role as collectors of wild foods produce relatively small quantities of food, but the variety thus added to the diet is probably more important nutritionally than the quantity would suggest. Women as gatherers work independently of men as hunters, and the exchange of forest foods between men and women is overlayed by the traditional screen of most hunting societies, in which the participants conceive their own system to be that men hunt for women, rather than an exchange of products between the sexes.

Although hunting is considered to be the primary occupation of all but elderly men, the Sharanahua do not spend even half their time hunting. During the month that I kept a record of hunting and the distribution of meat at the households of Basta, Zacharais, and Baiyakondi, the two most active hunters went out eleven times during the month. These three households included ten men at the time, half the number of men at Marcos. The cumulative odds for the success of all hunting attempts was 3 to 2, but individual odds varied from hunter to hunter. Presumably this was dependent upon the skill and luck of each hunter.

There was a greater difference between the number of times each man hunted than in the number of times each succeeded in bringing in game. Even when only the successful hunts are considered, the differences between individual hunters are still marked. The two men who hunted most were Basta and Tohukai. Both are mature men and both are sons-in-law of Zacharais. Basta, however, is the head of the largest household at Marcos, while Tohukai still lives in his father-in-law's household. At the time that the hunting record was kept, Basta's household contained one other man, Gustavo, six women, two adolescent girls, and seven children. Gustavo, Basta's son, hunted only four times during the month.

Zacharais is in his sixties. Although he still hunts, he does not hunt a great deal. He clears and plants gardens, however, for his wife and the daughter who is married to Tohukai. Tohukai left an older wife in another village to marry Yama-yahua, a beautiful and flirtatious young woman. They have been married for about eight years and have three children. This household contained only three adult women and four adult men, but Tohukai was the only active hunter in the household. Samuel, who was then living with his father, Zacharais, is a remarkably poor hunter by Sharanahua standards. In addition, during the period that the record was kept, he left Marcos for two weeks. The fourth man, Tararai, who had just married Samuel's daughter, is a skillful hunter, though he does not hunt frequently, and during the period that the hunting record was kept, he left Marcos for a week to work for a Peruvian in order to obtain a new shirt and pants.

Baiyakondi no longer hunts, and within his household, Buraya, his grandson, was the least active hunter of my sample. Buraya was then about eighteen years old and still unmarried. Sharafo, another inactive hunter in this household, is a Masti-nahua about twenty-two years old. He is married to Baiyakondi's granddaughter and has one child. Within this same house Iconahua hunted more often. He is in his early thirties, has two wives, and was living patrilocally at Baiyakondi's house since his first wife is a foreigner and his second an orphan. At the time I kept this record he was beginning to build his own house, and they moved out several months later with an Ama-huaca son-in-law.

It appears that the amount of hunting that a man does is affected in part by how often the other men of his household hunt. In addition, two other factors appeared crucial in affecting the number of times a man went hunting. First, the presence of a father-in-law who clears gardens for his (the son-in-law's) wife; and second, and perhaps the most important, a large number of women and children dependent upon his hunting effort.

It is important to keep in mind that these differences in hunting efforts are not reflected in individual differences in consumption, thus, Basta does not eat more meat than Gustavo; Zacharais does not eat less than Tohukai; Buraya eats as much as Iconahua. In addition to the men listed on the chart (see Appendix), it is informative to add two other men, Onsika and Ndaishiwaka. Onsika hunted more often and more successfully than any other man in the village. The father of five children, Onsika ate no better than anyone else. In contrast, Ndaishiwaka went hunting only twice during the four-week period. He and his family ate well and received more meat than several of the other families at Marcos.

These differences in consumption are directly related to the presence or absence of close kin within the village. Onsika is an Amahuaca married to Baido's daughter, and Baido has only one relative in Marcos. Ndaishiwaka's household regularly receives meat from Basta's household as well as from his younger brother's, Iconahua's.

There is no direct relationship between the amount of time and effort put into hunting and the amount of meat consumed by the hunter and his family. The community as a whole is made more secure by the traditional ideal that a hunter should share his game. There is no evidence, however, that Sharanahua are any more civic or community minded than members of our own society. The forced proximity of the *maloca* made it more difficult to avoid conformity to the sharing rule, but rewards for providing meat were also forthcoming.

Pride in hunting is a benefit to the society, and it is rewarded, less today than it used to be, by prestige. Prestige accrues to the generous hunter, not to one who hoards and hides his game. Prestige is not a vague goal at Marcos; it brings a definite reward, the possibility of gaining women as lovers and/

or wives. It is a common feature that the Sharanahua share with all tropical forest hunters: The successful hunter is usually the winner in the competition for women.

Today's secrecy about meat tends to reduce this reward and thereby reduces the incentives for hunting, producing reluctant and unenthusiastic hunters. Only during the infrequent special hunts, do young men have a chance to impress the women of the entire village with their skill at hunting, their virility as men.

At times, when there has been no meat in the village for three or four days, the women decide to send the men on a special hunt. They talk together and complain that there is no meat and the men are lazy. The young married women and the unmarried adolescent girls gather at Basta's house an hour before sundown. Their faces are painted and they have put on their best dresses and beads. They start at one end of Marcos and stop at each house, surrounding each man in turn. One or two women tug gently at his shirt or belt while they sing, "We are sending you to the forest to hunt, bring us back meat." They sing in Culina, a language considered exotic at Marcos. Tomuha, whose father was a Culina, usually leads the singing, although the other women know this song, as well as other Culina songs. They say that Tomuha is best at calling a special hunt.

Most men disregard the women, continuing their activities totally oblivious to their presence, even when the entire group encircles them. Only Shamarua and Taofaka look up to pull Koyo's hair and start a mock fight with Shimiri, trying to provoke the girls into sending them for game. The women sing to every man but Baiyakondi, who no longer hunts. If there are visitors from another village, they too are included. Their round of the village completed, the women separate and return to their own households.

The following morning, soon after sunrise, the men leave, traveling two or three in a canoe, generally heading downriver for one or two hours. They beach their canoes and split up, following different trails into the forest, some hunting alone, some in twos or threes. They head back to the canoes a little after noon. They wait for each other and usually return together. Two or three men may hunt longer if they have not yet found any game or if they have gone further into the forest in search of large game.

While the men are out hunting, the women prepare *mama,* a drink made from corn. They strip the kernels from the cob and roast them slowly on a piece of flattened metal placed over the fire. When the kernels are brown and crisp, they are placed in a large upright mortar made from a partially hollowed-out log. The corn is pounded to a fine powder and mixed with water. The women usually work cooperatively, one woman pounding the corn while another roasts the next batch. There are only three large mortars at Marcos and each is shared by several households.

Once the corn drink has been made and the daily chores of steaming manioc and gathering firewood are done, the women bathe in the river, put on their best clothes, and spend an hour or more painting careful designs on their faces and, sometimes, their legs.

Throughout the morning while the women work and decorate themselves, a certain amount of questioning and conversation goes on concerning which man each woman is "waiting for." The expression "waiting for" describes the fact that each woman has sent someone to hunt for her: Yawandi has sent Baido, Koyo waits for Shamarua, Tomuha waits for Sharafo, while Bashkoni says sorrowfully that Buraya is away upriver, and there is no one else to send since she has too many kin at Marcos, and a woman may not wait for her husband or for any brothers or fathers, sons, mothers' brothers, sons-in-law, fathers-in-law, or sisters' husband.

Tsatsa has sent Samuel time after time, and Yawandi has sent Baido for years. Shirimba sent Taofaka a few times while I was at Marcos, but one day I watched her hide behind my house to avoid him, and at the next special hunt she sent no one. Occasionally Tomuha has sent two men, but two women never wait for the same man. A few of the older women, such as Naikashu and Yawanini, help prepare the corn drink, but do not wait for anyone. They watch the games that follow the men's return from the forest, but they do not take part.

A short time before the men are expected to return, most of the young girls and some of the young women go into the forest to pick a plant called *nawawakusi*. This is a variety of stinging nettle which causes a red welt and intense itching for several hours when it is rubbed against the skin. The *nawawakusi* is kept in the house ready for later use against the men.

The men can be heard coming upriver when they are still a half hour from Marcos, and all the women who are taking part in the special hunt stand in front of Basta's house. The men walk solemnly up from the port, and silently each man drops the game he has shot on the ground before the waiting women and walks to his own house. Each woman picks up the animal that her partner has dropped and takes it to her own house and begins to prepare it. The men relax in their hammocks, eating pieces of manioc and cornmeal, waiting for the meat to be cooked. Once the meat has been skinned, cut up, and put to boil, each woman brings a pot of corn drink to her partner, setting it down next to his hammock. This drink is given even on the rare occasions when the man has failed to bring back any game.

As soon as the meat has cooked, everyone begins to eat. A great deal of visiting goes on, and invitations to eat are freely extended, so that people make the rounds of the village, eating at several houses in turn. The men compare this day's hunt to previous ones, remembering a good hunt when they brought in five peccaries and the last poor hunt when only monkeys could be found.

Everyone has barely finished eating when the young women burst into action with stalks of *nawawakusi* in their hands,

Games after the special hunt

trying to corner a young man. The men laugh, but they run, staying out of reach, hiding behind a house, until they are caught. Then they stand still, letting the girls triumphantly rub their chests, necks, and arms with the stinging nettle, which is said to give strength. The men finally seize some *nawawakusi* from the women and the chase becomes two sided with small groups of men and women in pursuit and retreat, laughing and shouting. The younger women are the favorite targets, and Koyo stops a moment to show off the red welts rising on her arms, complaining boastfully of how they hurt and itch. Children join in the chase, and, as among the adults, girls and boys are always opposed.

Two other games usually follow the *nawawakusi* chase, beginning in the large cleared area in front of Basta's house. In one, a man places a fiber rope around the waist of one of the women (not necessarily his special hunt partner), while she fixes the same kind of rope around his shoulder and under one arm. They both strain to dislodge the other's footing and to toss their opponent to the ground. Sometimes one or more people come running to add their weight; women help women; men help men. In the second game, a man takes a short piece of sugar cane, walks provocatively past several women, taps them teasingly with the cane, and runs away. One or more women will pursue him, reaching to grab the piece of sugar cane. Men help each other by passing or tossing the cane, and women help each other by blocking the men's path.

The effort involved in these games is enormous, considering that they are carried out in a clearing, under the afternoon sun, some ten degrees from the equator. When one asks why they are playing, the answer is, *"nami ichapa, no fusino,"* "there's lot of meat, let's play." By about five o'clock the games stop, and everyone goes to bathe in the river—partly to cool off and partly to sooth the welts caused by the stinging nettle.

The special hunt usually results in more meat in the village than a normal day's hunt, although it can be unproductive.

There was one special hunt in which monkeys were the only game, and they amounted to less meat than on a good normal hunting day, even though more individual animals were brought in. During two special hunts I made a count of all the game brought into the village. In the first, the total was two collared peccaries, one deer, five monkeys; in the second, the total was eight monkeys. For the ten men of my sample, the amount brought in during a third special hunt was three white-lipped peccaries, one monkey, and one bird.

The social pressure of the special hunt, the line of women painted and waiting, makes young men try hard to succeed. On one occasion, Buraya and Sharafo, usually two of the least active hunters at Marcos, searched the forest till darkness fell, risking the spirits, but returning with three large peccaries. Basta and Zacharais, secure in their position as heads of large households returned without meat one time. They beached their canoes, however, at a different port rather than run the gamut of waiting women, and they walked to their houses by a different trail, looking downcast and angry.

During the special hunts there are important shifts in the pattern of distributing meat. Meat is given directly outside of the household, rather than to a wife, a mother-in-law, or a mother within the hunter's household. Since the special hunt partner must be someone outside the circle of close relatives, this means that meat is given to a household which is not among the usual recipients of distribution from the man's household. In the normal hunt, game is often distributed to at least one other household, while meat received in a special hunt is not distributed, rather, invitations to eat are freely given by members of each household. It is the only time that young women are in a position to issue invitations to their sisters and cousins. The shift in the distribution pattern equalizes available hunting skills as men hunt for households other than their own.

A reverse special hunt was held once in which the men sent the women out to fish for them. A visitor from another village

sang to send them off because the men at Marcos had never
done this. The women left in the morning, canoeing upriver to
a small stream, which is a favorite spot for drug fishing. The men
did not arrange to make or obtain anything with which to
reciprocate. They went to collect *nawawakusi*, however, painted
their faces, and made decorative hats. They waited for the
women at the same place, in front of Basta's house.

The women returned a little after noon and marched up
the path from the port to the house. They were trying to carry
it off with the same seriousness that the men display, but they
were embarrassed and unsuccessful at hiding their sheepish
smiles and giggles. The fish were dropped in a pile in front of
the men, and each man picked up the leaf-wrapped packet of
fish that his partner had brought. The partnerships were the
same as those of the usual special hunt. During the afternoon
the men inaugurated the *nawawakusi* chasing, but the usual
games followed. This reverse special hunt was held on November 11, 1966, following special hunts on November 8 and 10,
1966. This suggests that the men may have felt that the
women were sending them to hunt too often and tried to put
them in their place by making them feel foolish. If this was
the motive it apparently failed since the women sent them out
again the following day.

Special hunts are not usually so frequent. The beginning
of the rainy season, however, is both a good time for hunting
and, perhaps, a temptation to the women. During the dry season,
from the end of April to mid-October, several men are likely to
be out of the village on any day, hunting jaguars and turtle
eggs far upriver, or working for a few days in their gardens.
When I asked the women why they had not called a special
hunt, despite their complaints of no meat, they told me that
too many men were away from Marcos, and they would wait
until they returned.

The women attempted one special hunt for fish rather than
game. They sang the men off in the morning. When the men
returned, the chasing with *nawawakusi* was carried out, but

there were no games afterward. This took place also in November and never again while I was at Marcos. The rainy season ends the period of drug fishing, and it may be that the reason for momentarily placing fishing on a level with hunting was that there would be no good catches of fish again until April.

Children occasionally hold special hunts in imitation of their elders. The girls send the boys out and the boys come back with fish, occasionally a bird, or some gathered palm nuts. The girls are painted and dressed in their best and usually present the boys with a small pot of banana drink, which is much more easily prepared than the corn drink. These play special hunts are generally brief events, taking place late in the afternoon, ending with dancing by evening. Sometimes the boys dance and the girls threaten them with lit torches.

Women take part in the adult special hunts while girls play at the children's. The dividing line is obvious: Girls past puberty are included with women, married or single; girls not yet pubescent are children, even though some of them are married. For men, of course, the line demarcating boyhood from adulthood is not as clearcut, and in the special hunt the women make the decision of whom to include. Adolescent boys, such as Shandi and Dikandi are not included, they are still lumped with the children.

The choice of partners in the special hunts is usually a choice of lovers, and for this reason neither children nor close kin are possible partners. The teasing and the provocation of the special hunt games are symbolically sexual and, despite the discretion of most love affairs at Maroos, some flirtations are obvious, and they coincide with the partnerships of the special hunt. The women of Basta's household told me of their own love affairs and those of others, and they usually chose one of their lovers as a partner.

Put at its crudest, the special hunt symbolizes an economic structure in which meat is exchanged for sex. This is neither a "natural" nor "rational" exchange since women produce at least as much of the food supply at Marcos, and a rational exchange would consist of viewing the economy as an exchange of women's production for men's. Certainly there is no evidence that women are naturally less interested in sex or more interested in meat than men are. This is a culturally produced socioeconomic system in which sex is the incentive for hunting, and a man who is known to be a good hunter has a better chance of gaining wives or mistresses. The circular logic of the system is that men compete against other men because women are scarce. Women are scarce because sex is not free, but must be won, and because some men have more than one wife. A man with one wife is still competing and part of the reason for wanting more than one wife is to prove that one is a man. In the daily hunt, secrecy about meat prevents young men from demonstrating their prowess as hunters since only members of their own households know which man has provided the meat. The special hunt gives an opportunity for men to demonstrate their hunting skill to women other than their wives. It is a dramatic portrayal of the exchange between the sexes, which structures daily interactions between men and women.

This structure appears to be common to most tropical forest people, and it is expressed in a myth which, in various forms is widespread among these cultures. The central theme describes a love affair between a tapir and a woman. The husband eventually discovers his wife and her tapir lover, kills the tapir, and, in many versions, forces his wife to eat or copulate with the tapir's penis after which she dies. This theme appears in two Sharanahua myths (see Chapters 7 and 9) with additional complications. In this myth the tapir, the largest game animal of the forest, is literally connected with women. Man in the role of the hunter kills his rival, who becomes meat, eliminates freely given sex from the universe, and sets up an antagonistic relationship to women, in which the hunter must win women by killing game.

A system in which women are an incentive does not lead

to a friendly, easygoing relationship between men and women. Women look for the good hunter, the good provider, not for companionship. The prestige system carries a sting: The good hunter is the virile man, but the hunter with little skill or bad luck does not find sympathy. When children scream at their mothers, *"Nami pipai!"* "I want to eat meat!" their mothers' reply, *"Nami yamai,"* "There is no more meat," is a goad that women aim at their husbands, provoking them to hunt again, implying that they are less than men since there is no more meat.

A man may spend hours in the forest. One day Basta returned empty handed, tired, muddy from wading through swampy ground and picking ticks off his body. No words of sympathy were forthcoming, and I asked Yawandi why she and Bashkondi were painting their faces. She replied in a voice that carried clearly to the hammock where Basta rested alone, "We want to paint, there's no meat, let's eat penises!" On other days as well I have suspected that women paint their faces as an unspoken challenge to the men. In one version of the Sharanahua tapir myth, the tapir and then the hunter attract the woman by throwing genipa fruits, the fruit which yields black face paint.

When men return from hunting with nothing to show, their wives sometimes accuse them of meeting a woman to make love rather than hunt. Men in turn suspect their wives of carrying on love affairs while they search the forest for game. Both are often correct. Neither husbands nor wives are supposed to be jealous of the love affairs involved in the special hunt. In general, jealousy is considered to be a bad trait in a wife or a husband, and I have heard both men and women complain that they are unlucky to have a jealous spouse. It is seldom a reason for divorce, for "throwing away" one's spouse, nor is it sufficient reason to end a love affair, but it provokes quarrels between couples.

Yawandi has told me that men used to be "angry," that long ago they punished their wives for infidelity. I asked if that included love affairs with husband's brother or her *bimbiki*, and she said no, even then these were permissible lovers, and husbands were not supposed to be jealous. The terms for husband's brother and brother's wife are *"fakupa"* and *"fakuwa."* These terms refer to specific individuals who are related in this way through marriage. Their relationship falls within the category of *bimbiki*, "potential spouse."

Ipo, after her marriage to Iconahua, used to come to my house while I was working with Ndaishiwaka, her *fakupa*. They laughed and flirted and led me to ask, at a different time, if it was usual to make love to one's *fakuwa*, brother's wife. Ndaishiwaka said no, that one might "play" with her and that she could give food to her *fakupa*, but that sexual intercourse was forbidden. When I told Yawandi this version she laughed and told me he lied, and several women added that he had been sleeping with his other *fakuwa* for years. A brother's wife is often an actual *bimbiki* of both men, or if a foreigner, is still an allowable sexual partner.

The hidden competition at Marcos is between "brothers," men of the same descent group. They pursue the same women since they share the same incest taboos, and any woman available to one brother is a possible wife or mistress for the other. Love affairs between *fakupa* and *fakuwa*, husband's brother and brother's wife, may ease the competition or strengthen it. The availability of *fakuwa* as a sexual partner eases the competition among brothers for wives, but when women are perceived as scarce, and one man is far more successful than the other, the rivalry among brothers may become intense. In particular, a distant "brother," with whom there are few interactions, becomes a tapir-rival for one's wife.

This competition is built into the structure of the village, and it is overlayed both by loyalty to one's kinsmen and the often friendly relationship between men who have grown up together. It is further contained by the absolute prohibition of any open competitive behavior between men and finds expression instead in contempt for foreigners and male solidarity in the battle of the sexes.

This complex of behavior that is related to hunting is part of learning the sex role of a man. The changes of the last twenty-five years are gradually shifting roles and expectations, but the role of a man is still first and foremost that of a hunter. A small boy's first toy is a bow and arrow, a tiny version of his father's five and a half foot bow. Three year olds gravely stalk butterflies, their kin beaming with pride. Six year olds beg their older brothers to make them bows and arrows, and boys of ten and older are experts at manufacturing two-foot bows and short, straight arrows. Men make three types of arrows for hunting: broad, lance-shaped bamboo points for big game; barbed hardwood points for monkeys and birds; and a three-pointed barbed, hardwood point for fishing. Nowadays a man must also find a way to earn the money to buy a shotgun and shells.

Skill at hunting, especially with bow and arrows, seems to depend on starting young. Most men are good hunters, though some are better than others. Samuel is the only really poor hunter at Marcos, and it may be related to the fact that he spent a few years in early childhood living with a Peruvian. His own father was dead, and the Peruvian adopted him. When Yawanini, his mother, married Zacharais, his father's brother, they took Samuel back to the *maloca*.

I asked Yawandi once why Samuel was a poor hunter. She replied that when Samuel went to hunt peccary, the peccaries ran away; and when Samuel hunted for capybara, they fled. Samuel missed out on the early learning in which fathers encourage their sons' efforts with tiny bows and arrows. This would lead to being the poorest among the group of older boys who spend their days hunting birds and frogs. I have never dared ask Samuel since questioning a man's lack of skill at hunting is equivalent to discussing his lack of virility. I believe that Samuel's failure as a hunter is not primarily due to a lack of the physical skills but rather to his lack of understanding of the complex of rivalry and sexual antagonism that is an integral part of hunting at Marcos.

Little boys are taught to be sexually aggressive and little girls are taught to provoke and protect themselves. A mother laughs with pride at her two-year-old son's imitation of the motions of sex or her small daughter's pout and slap at a teasing man. Three-year-old Comafo was brought to my house by one of the women who take care of him. Old Baido laughingly pretended to grab the woman, and Comafo stood up fiercely and aimed the conventional Sharanahua "fuck you" gesture at Baido. Comafo's grandfather pounded his chest and beamed proudly at his small grandson. Everyone else laughed, and Comafo cried. Comafo has learned a basic social fact, that other men are his competitors over women, and this is why Basta, his grandfather, was proud. Comafo has not yet learned to conceal his anger, but adult laughter will soon teach him. Samuel may have failed to learn the relationship between competition for women and hunting skills as the way of winning them. Samuel has mistresses, but he is unable to take a second wife since he gives in to Ifama's jealousy. A successful man at Marcos need not pay attention to his wife's feelings.

In most ways in everyday life the sexes are evenly matched at Marcos, but they are matched against each other in a semi-playful, semi-hostile battle. Sharanahua women are strong, but the men usually succeed in tossing them in the games of the special hunt. The women, however usually succeed in coercing the men to hunt for them. Only once in the time I spent at Marcos did they fail. This was an evening when many visitors had come from Boca de Curanja, and almost all the men were together drinking strong manioc beer at Basta's house. The young women sang to them, but no one hunted. Unlike a usual evening when men are scattered in their own households, sitting alone or playing with a child, the men were able to present a solid front.

They could argue that no one would lose face or come out ahead since no one would hunt.

Sharanahua women are rarely frightened by any man, unless he is drunk, but a group of men together are viewed as dangerous. The women say, "We'll be raped," and will not join such a group. I never was told of a case of rape, but the threat keeps women "in their place," from taking part in activities that are seen as male, and from attempting to push the men too hard. Women express feelings of antagonism toward men by attacking them with *nawawakusi*. On one occasion the men had been drinking heavily the day before, and by early evening were extremely drunk. Several fights were threatened, and one man was so drunk that he fell off the floor of his house, a four-foot drop to the ground. The next day his wife led a bunch of women in an attack on the men with *nawawakusi*. She attacked several men while several other women attacked her husband.

The men's threat of rape and the women's attack with *nawawakusi* are symbolic statements demonstrating the structure of male and female social groupings. The stability of the male-female relationship, based as it is on mutual social and economic dependence allows for the open expression of hostility. There are other hostilities at Marcos and their expression would widen cracks and break up the village whereas the battle of the sexes provides a village-wide loyalty. The ritualization of male solidarity in antagonism to female solidarity puts strain on the only relationship in this society that can stand it. This combination of same sex solidarity and antagonism to the other sex prevents the households from becoming tightly closed units. The competition between "brothers" is relieved by their moving to different households, as Moon in the myth leaves his brother, in obedience to the matrilocal rule, and this rule prevents the patrilineal descent groups from solidifying and separating out from the village.

6

MARCOS

Fishing and Agriculture, Cooperation Between Men and Women

At Marcos the dry season begins about the end of April and lasts into October. Although it rains in the dry season too, the almost daily rains stop, the river begins to go down, and the silt-laden water of the Purús clears. During the rainy months a cup of water from the river is mud brown, and one must wait for the silt to settle before drinking. While the Purús is a "white" river, whose waters are never perfectly clear, in the dry season one can fill a pot with river water and drink it immediately.

Hunting continues throughout the dry season, but fishing becomes a more frequent and more important activity than in the rainy season for a few months as the streams become shallow enough to use fish drugs. Men and women work together, and members of several households usually go out together. Men cut up the woody stalks of *tsika, barbasco,* or women strip the leaves and berries of *pooikama, huaca,* and pound them in the mortar.

Casha, the old shaman, takes a turn, thrusting his hips back and forth as he thuds the pestle into the mortar in a comic pantomime of the act of sex. Field cans are filled with the sodden green pulp, and women grab small pots of cooked manioc and bananas, and ten to twenty people go down the paths to their canoes. Fasha avoids her mother's eyes and the chore of watching out for her younger brother by jumping into Bashkondi's canoe.

The older boys, like the men, take fish spears, long wooden poles with two strong nails embedded in their tips, and distribute themselves among the various canoes, generally avoiding their fathers'. Boys are almost the equal of men at drug fishing, and having different members of a household in more than one canoe tends to ensure that every household will have fish if it is a good day.

We pole upriver, an hour away to Chuspi, a stream off to our left as we go. A month ago in June, when we tried to fish, we found Chuspi still a ten-foot-wide river, deep and with a strong current. Even continuing up into its small tributary streams, the water was still so high and deep that there was no point in throwing in the drug. It would be too diluted to have any effect. In July, though, the rivers are low, and as we reach the beaches at every curve of the Purús, everyone, but the two men poling the canoe, jumps out and walks across the beach to lighten the load and speed the trip. Yawandi walks at the edge of the beach, looking for *iwi shano*, "sand rays," flat like the larger sting rays, but harmless and good to eat. At Chuspi, now that the river is down, we have to pull the canoe into the river bed since silt has half blocked the channel.

Chuspi is down to five feet in width, with logs across the water and low vines and branches entangled at chest height. At places we push and tug the canoes through—the depth varies from two to ten feet. We duck to the bottom of the canoe so as not to get hit by the branches. We reach a spot where one canoe continues with all the cans of the fish drug, and the rest of us wait downstream. The cans full of pounded leaves are emptied into the canoe, the drug is mixed with water, and the canoe load is then shoveled into the stream with the broad paddle. Only a few minutes pass as we keep our canoes still and watch the water. A few fish start to rise, momentarily suffocated by the drug's effect, which reduces their intake of oxygen, and we go racing up for them, the men and boys with spears held poised, the women scanning for small fish they can take with their hands.

Everyone starts yelling as bigger fish appear near the surface, and they are stabbed before they again come to their senses and dive deep. The canoes chase up and down the narrow stream, the women sit, grabbing the tiny two-inch fish that lie stunned or dead on the surface. Men and boys stand, stabbing with their spears. Some of the boys use the three-pronged wooden fishing arrow as a spear, throwing it and then leaning out or jumping onto the bank to recover it. The canoes start heading slowly downstream, but rush back up again as someone sights one more fish. Only when there has been not the slightest indication of a fish moving for a while do we finally stop searching and head for the mouth of Chuspi.

Through all the excitement of watching, screaming, stabbing, pulling the fish off the spear, killing it with a hard blow of a machete if it is big enough to bite or leap out over the side, everyone keeps track of which canoe got which fish. The person who sights the fish first usually gets it, even if someone else has stabbed it. Sometimes in the rush to get a fish off the spear, it is simpler to let someone else remove it. These are now returned and sometimes two almost identical fish are exchanged between canoes. Though each person keeps the fish he has taken in his own basket or can, some are shared between the people in one canoe, and on the trip back downstream boys dump their fish into their fathers' tall cans and often ride back in their canoes.

Downriver is a fast ride, paddling lightly and letting the current take the canoe. Women start gutting and cleaning the fish, scaling them and dipping them into the river to wash them. As we go up the paths at Marcos, we tell people, *"Shima ichapa!"* "There's lots of fish!" Naikashu wraps the tiny fish in leaves tied with a fiber and puts them in the fire with a few large cat fish, roasting in their armor, and flat *boca chica* with diagonal slashes breaking up the innumerable bones of the flesh. Yawandi and Tarani clean the rest of the fish, as Bashkondi chops them in large chunks and puts them to boil.

Sometimes a small group will fish in a stream nearer to Marcos, walking an hour through the forest and wading up a shallow stream. I go with Zacharais and Yawanini, Bashkondi, Yawandi, and the inevitable bunch of children, magically protecting our feet from the sting rays that lie in the mud banks by brushing our legs with branches. Where the stream begins to deepen, Zacharais dams it up with thatch and pounds the stalks of *tsika* into the stream, but the water is too deep and too fast moving and a handful of two-inch fish is the whole catch.

A group of women sometimes fish by themselves, walking far along a narrow stream, stopping and peeling open each piece of sunken hollow bamboo. Some are filled with mud, but in others there are small shrimp or a strange catfish with a bunched appendage on each side of its head. They look to me like two hands, but Naikashu refers to them as hair and exclaims, "Ishki, Ishki *ishta!*" "Dear, little Ishki!" and puts it in her basket.

The women find a good spot and empty the basket of *pooikama* and wade through the stream, grabbing and slashing with their knives. The fish are fairly small, an eight-inch is one of the largest, and they are cleaned and wrapped in leaves to take back while Naikashu cooks most of the smaller fish on a small fire by the side of the stream, and we roast manioc in the fire and eat the fish with salt that has been carried along in a small leaf.

As we begin the walk back through the stream, Yawanini shrieks, "Ari!" and grabs her foot. It is streaming blood from the hole left by a sting ray. Bashkondi and Yawandi rush to get leaves and squeeze them onto Yawanini's foot as Naikashu holds it. Within minutes Yawanini is shaking convulsively. Naikashu says she is drunk with the pain, and she moans, "Ari! Ari!" The women heat a pot of water and fill it with a special leaf, squeezing the hot green liquid into the wound. Ruapa walks through this scene looking for game. He stops and searches the stream bed for the sting ray. He finds it and cuts off the one-inch long stiff stinger, which is thrown into the pot of leaves. The rest of the sting ray is put with the other fish. Yawanini is an old woman and the pain is excruciating, but she walks the slippery, now ascending, now descending path back to the village, occasionally being carried on Bash-kondi's back.

Men sometimes fish alone with bows and arrows, circling around the edge of the lake on foot or, with a companion, canoeing close to the shore. Three men at Marcos have learned from the Peruvians to make fish nets in the last few years. These are used in the lake, and though the *tarafa,* the Peruvian fish net, only catches one fish at a time, the lake is rich especially in the dry season, and a man can depend upon catching two or three good size *boca chica.* A few men buy metal harpoon heads from the traders to fish the Purús itself or to try for *paiche,* the largest freshwater fish in the world. *Paiche* are rarely taken, however, even with a harpoon, and I have only seen two at Marcos. Another innovation is to fish the lake at night when fish come in close to shore, shining a flashlight, preferably mine since batteries are expensive, and spearing the fish.

Except for bows and arrows, these other techniques depend upon trade and are, therefore, still secondary in frequency and importance to drug fishing. Occasionally groups of men or groups of women fish separately. Usually though, fishing with drugs at Marcos is most successful when it is undertaken by a large group with men to handle the canoes and spear the fish and with women to kill the fish once they are taken from the spear, and to grab the small fish, and to clean them.

Hunting carries no taboos, but fishing with drugs may not be done by a woman who is menstruating or by a man who has had sexual intercourse within the past three days. If the taboo is broken, it is believed that the fish will not be affected by the drug. Yawandi was angry one afternoon when, despite the efforts of a large group of people using fish drugs in a stream that had not been fished for months, only a few tiny fish died, and it turned out that Onsika had had intercourse with his wife the night before.

These taboos seem understandable as an attempt to symbolically eliminate the sexual antagonism that is basic to hunting in order to allow the cooperation between men and women, which is desirable for fishing. Perhaps it is this temporary reduction of antagonism and competition that makes fishing expeditions a gay and exciting enterprise. Neither sex can accuse the other of failure where both are participant, and most fishing trips are at least partly successful. This analysis seems supported by the story of Dika, a somewhat confusing myth, which derives the drug for fishing from the excrement of the tapir, thus making fishing a secondary development from the hunting structure. Dika appear in several stories as a malevolent trickster, and in this story he revenges himself on "first woman" for refusing his sexual advances.

First woman went to defecate and came upon the tracks of a tapir. Dika wiped out the tracks and changed the tapir into a huge black man, who said to the woman, "Your husband is dead. I want you."

At first the woman refused but then succumbed, and they copulated over and over until she became pregnant with a huge baby. The tapir-man said, "Let's go fishing." He used his own excrement (*pooi*) for the fish drug (*pooi-kama*).

The woman left her human child at home, and when she and the tapir-man returned laden with fish, her daughter was covered with tapir-lice. The woman sat on the child's hammock, and, using his nose, her unborn tapir-baby copulated with the child. The woman's *fakupa,* her husband's younger brother, killed the tapir-man. The tapir-baby at his birth split his mother open, and she died.

This story of "first woman" describes a self-sufficient and impossible social and economic unit in which the woman is directly involved with the tapir, her unborn son commits incest with his own sister, and the tapir, the symbol of wild animals, produces the fish drug. Yawandi's version of this myth appears to incorporate a symbolic shorthand. The killing of the tapir by the younger brother seems symbolic of the hunting structure in which men kill their tapir-rivals by hunting game to win women, and "first woman" is a potential mistress for her husband's brother. Fishing complicates the story, however, since the young man cannot fish with an antagonistic woman, but must find a cooperative partner. Therefore, in contrast to most tapir-myths, the hunter does not kill the woman to set up the battle of the sexes. Instead, the product of the relationship between women and game, the tapir-baby, eliminates this woman. Thus, at the end of the myth what remains are game, fish poison, and a father-daughter dyad. That is, the baby-tapir is descended from a human, as peccaries are descended from humans and become game in the myth of the origin of the peccary. The father-daughter dyad is composed of the woman's husband's brother and her daughter since brother's daughter is also a daughter.

This is the nonsexual relationship that is the building block of the household and a prerequisite for cooperation between men and women. Hunting relies on an exchange, a semi-hostile game in which men hunt tapirs to get sexual rewards. Fishing and agriculture, which are related through the planting of fish drugs, requires that men and women work together; hence the sexual relationship is played down and the asexual relationship of father and daughter is emphasized.

Agriculture, like fishing, demands a synchronization of the

work of men and women. In addition, agricultural work is an investment of time and effort; a man will not work hard for two months clearing land without the security of knowing that women will harvest and prepare the food. The sexual incentive for hunting is logical since hunting is a brief but recurring task as sex is a brief but recurring need. The ease with which marriages are established and broken at Marcos fits well with the basic hunting economy, but a more stable relationship is essential for the responsibilities of agriculture. The myth of Dika ends with the same relationship as the myth of the jaguar's wife. The *upa-achi* relationship, which is the central tie of the extended matrilocal household. A father and daughter each married to a member of another *upa-achi* dyad, son-in-law and mother-in-law (the son-in-law's father's sister).

Men clear gardens for their wives and for their married daughters. A manioc garden is cleared for each wife and daughter; a plantain garden is sometimes cleared for all of them, sometimes for the first wife and a daughter. Young, unmarried men seldom make gardens or help their fathers. Sons-in-law begin to garden for their wives only when children have stabilized the marriage. Their gardens are made in the general area of their father-in-law's clearing, facilitating the cooperation of the women of the household.

Women have gardens as long as their fathers or their husbands are alive. So that Yawandi, though single, has gardens that Basta has made, while Momu, husbandless and fatherless with three children, forever plagued her sisters and cousins in the village for manioc and plantains, and was obsequious and pitiful, searching always for a husband. Everyone laughed and said that Momu had had too many lovers and too many husbands, and no one would stay with her. The last year I was at Marcos Momu's daughter had married and borne a child, and Momu's son-in-law was beginning to clear gardens.

Men usually work alone, clearing their gardens; another

man may be working a garden nearby, but each does the heavy work alone. In June men work consistently several mornings a week, returning with headaches from the hot sun.

Old men like Casha and Baiyakondi clear gardens near the village on land which has been planted recently before, on which the secondary growth is not high. It is more work and more days of clearing, but it takes less strength than bringing down the tall trees of an unused plot. Basta and Ndaishiwaka pride themselves on picking good high land with tall trees, the most productive land for manioc and maize, which may lie an hour's walk from Marcos, or half an hour away by canoe. Each year land further from Marcos is cleared, and last summer Ndaishiwaka and Iconahua each built small temporary houses on the beach in which to stay while they cleared their new gardens.

Dry season is the only time of year when men spend a good deal of time at agricultural work. Most of the clearing is completed by the end of June or mid-July, and the gardens are left, with the cut-down branches drying out and protecting the thin tropical soil from the ravenous sun.

The silt layed down as the Purús recedes from its rainy season banks is used for planting peanuts, some maize, and watermelons. No clearing is necessary, and women carry out these tasks. In the past, however, before the Sharanahua lived by the river, peanuts and maize were only planted in gardens which men had cleared, and watermelons were unknown. Women also plant cotton in small gardens which their husbands have cleared, or on the edges of the manioc gardens.

Burning starts in late August. As one stands by the river, looking downstream, columns of smoke rise high. Fathers go with their daughters to burn off the gardens: Zacharais with Bashkondi and Yamayahua, Basta and Yawandi, Ndaishiwaka and Ishamba. Younger men occasionally help their *ania*, their sister's husbands or their wife's brothers, who will reciprocate.

I asked to join Basta and Yawandi in their canoe, and as we went down the path to the river I noticed that they were both painted as were the small children tagging along to watch. The paint had been applied carelessly, not in a precise pattern, but just the basic element of the standard design, a red streak from the corner of the mouth across the cheeks to the lobe of the ear. I ran my fingers across Rombu's paint and streaked my own face since the painting that day had a ritual feeling. When I asked Yawandi about it, she told me it was to insure a good burn.

We poled half an hour upstream to the garden, where Basta and Yawandi lit torches and started far away at one end. They walked slowly forward, spaced far apart, lighting the dry branches that lay all over the ground. The fire burned slowly and the smoke started to rise, and the heat rising forced a wind into the faces of the children and myself. We backed away from the heat, and the sound of the fire increased. Basta and Yawandi climbed over and around the branches, spreading the fire with their torches. They were dripping with perspiration; the combined heat of the sun and the fire drove us, the watchers, toward the end of the garden and down the path to the river, and we waited for them by the canoe.

As we paddled back downriver to Marcos, I asked if it had been a good burn. Yawandi said, "No." I asked why it had not burned well, fearing that my presence might be blamed, but Yawandi explained that there had not been enough people to burn it thoroughly. During both of the dry seasons that I have spent at Marcos, the first rains of the rainy season began within two days of burning the gardens, quick thunderstorms which, according to the women, encourage the turtles to lay their eggs.

A few days after a field has been burned, the men plant manioc, placing a five-inch piece of the branch at a slanting angle into the soil below the ashes. Maize is planted next, then plantain cuttings, each in a separate garden, with a few potatoes and squashes interplanted with the maize. A few men have begun to plant rice, originally purchased from the Peruvians, and it is becoming a popular addition to the diet. Once the crops are planted, men are free of their gardens.

Plantains and bananas produce fruit after a year and a half and continue bearing for years. Eight different varieties are growing at Marcos and more are known. Some are considered especially good for *mania butsa,* some are true bananas, eaten uncooked, sweet, and sugary.

Maize grows rapidly, and the crop planted by the women along the beaches may be harvested within three months. The maize planted later in the gardens will ripen before the next dry season. A few early ears are eaten green, but most are allowed to ripen fully, turning hard and golden so the kernels can be roasted and eaten, or pounded to make *mama,* the corn drink, or wrapped in a leaf and roasted to make a bread-like dish.

Manioc is the staple without which a meal is incomplete. If one is offered a snack of an egg or a tiny piece of fish one reaches first for a piece of steamed manioc to eat with it. Manioc may be harvested after six months, but it is best after a year and a half to two years. After two years it is ideal for making a drink called *puti,* "manioc beer."

Weeding, the every other day harvesting of manioc, and the approximately twice weekly harvesting of plantains and bananas are part of the work of women throughout the year. Co-wives, sisters, daughters and their mother, generally work together. Occasionally they share the produce of their gardens, if crops in one are not yet ripe. More often the women of two households go together to their gardens and return each to her own house with the harvest. Each woman stores her own baskets of maize and peanuts, and Yawandi occasionally envies the quantity that Bashkondi has been able to harvest, while

Ifama with Yawandi preparing mild manioc beer
The two girls are Ahuiyumba and Fasha

Bashkondi must ask Naikashu for maize when the special hunt occurs, and a pot of corn drink must be made.

There is an admission that I am sorry to make—I have never watched the women work in their manioc gardens. I have walked through gardens while people were weeding or cutting down a bunch of bananas. I have waited in the canoe while Naikashu, Ifama, and small Shomoiya harvested manioc. Partly, it may be due to sheer inertia, the unpleasantness of working under the heat of the sun, but in searching my ethnographic

Ifama and her youngest daughter, Shomoiya

conscience, I conclude that I was responding to the women's dislike of having any but a close kinswoman, sister, mother, or daughter, take part in the harvesting of manioc. I mention this both to allow for the possibility of a lack in my data, and also to suggest that women's ties to their kinswomen and their gardens are a significant factor in their lives as well as a means of making the theft of garden produce difficult.

I have gone with the women of Basta's household to harvest watermelons along the beach, and once Naikashu noticed a footprint, belonging, she said, to Momu, a woman of a distant household. The women were angry since the watermelons they had expected to find ripe on the vines were gone, and there was nothing they could do since Momu was not their kin.

For women the kinship relationships of sister, mother, and daughter, are close and permanent. Even when a daughter's husband sets up an independent household, the tie between daughter and her parents holds the households together. The importance of the mother-daughter tie is contradicted in part by the descent rule that places all children in their father's descent group not their mother's. The father-daughter tie is stressed in the myths, the mother-daughter tie is continually apparent in every day's activities. This contradiction appears as a major theme in the myth of Kapa, the Squirrel Spirit.

"Listen," said Baiyakondi, "I will tell you the story of Squirrel Spirit:

Everyone had gone away to eat dirt, except for two nubile girls who stayed with their sick mother. There was nothing to eat so the two girls went to get shrimp and small crayfish, while their mother rolled clay to make pots. As they were going they heard a strange sound. It was Squirrel playing with the corn he had raised. The girls saw Squirrel as a handsome young man with long hair and small eyes. He asked the sisters where they were going and followed along.

Now Squirrel had his long stick, and he told them he would get many fish for them. They were sitting with their backs to him, and he made two deep holes by stabbing with his stick, and the water emptied from the stream. He told the sisters that there were lots of fish, and they filled two baskets with catfish and sting rays. Then they turned away, and when they next looked at the stream, the water had risen. "Let's go, younger sister, we will eat." And they brought the food to their mother who was hungry. All their mother's brothers had gone away to eat dirt.

They told their mother about Squirrel, and she told them to bring Squirrel to her and he would be her son-in-law. They brought him and showed him where their father used to have his gardens, which now were empty. Squirrel worked all night, and when they got up they saw manioc and corn, lots of it as it used to be. Squirrel stored the ripe corn, and they were all happy and went to tell the people who were eating dirt. In the morning the mother-in-law went nearby to urinate, and a branch of manioc scratched her eyebrow.

Squirrel kept on making gardens for his two wives and he had many children, but he did not go hunting. He planted potatoes and bananas for his children. One day Squirrel's young brother-in-law, his *ania,* came to where Squirrel was clearing a field and he started to play with Squirrel's fire-making stick. "Stop messing with my stick, brother-in-law, what you are doing is bad." But his brother-in-law kept playing with the stick and it opened and a flame burst out, and soon his brother-in-law was all burned. Squirrel heard the fire and ran over—his stick was open and it burned his hair before he managed to get it closed.

"Why did you do it, brother-in-law," he said, "I have told you so often!" His brother-in-law's bones were all cinders, his flesh was gone. Squirrel got two palm fruit seeds for eyes, and fruit silk for hair, and tied up the bones. Then he squeezed leaf juice and cured him. Squirrel warned him not to tell his mother the truth, but to say instead that he was feverish. His brother-in-law told his mother what had happened, and he died of fever.

Squirrel stayed a long time and made many gardens, but he told his wives not to come to where he worked—there mouse, *ponchana,* paca, and other rodents were helping him. But his father-in-law came and thought the rodents were stealing the corn, so he chased them away and they never returned. Squirrel asked, "How could you do that? My kin [*unwu yura*], your affinals [*raisi*] were planting the corn." His father-in-law replied that no one had told him. Squirrel grew lots of corn, and when his mother-in-law saw it she was very happy and filled her baskets.

One day Squirrel went hunting, but one of his wives

did not want to go since she planned to meet her lover. So Squirrel went to the forest with all their children and his other wife and killed a spider monkey. When the children slept, Squirrel changed into a bat and went to find his wife with her lover in the hammock. Squirrel bit the hammock rope so it fell and the lover said, "Your bad-eyed husband made a bad hammock rope. Let's go by the fire."

They lay on the mat by the fire, and the bat bit off the lover's penis and carried it away. Then Squirrel took strong monkey fat and mixed it with the sliced penis and wrapped it up, telling the children he was making it for their mother, but warning his other wife not to eat it. Then he brought it to his bad wife. He asked her why she was crying and she replied that his *rawi* (his wife's sister's husband) had been bitten by a huge bat and had died.

Squirrel said, "Eat this, then we will both weep. I wrapped this fat for you." So she ate the monkey fat all wrapped up and fell sick and dizzy from eating the penis." "Get me water, I'm thirsty," she said. "I'm thirsty and I can't get up."

"I won't fetch water, get it yourself," said Squirrel. "You are sick because your lover is making you sick. You have eaten his penis." And he left, making bat noises, and the woman died.

One can look at the story of Squirrel as a statement of the complexity and difficulty of combining the various forms of labor necessary for subsistence by means of the social structuring of relationships within the extended household. At the beginning of Squirrel, there are two girls and their mother, who have been left behind as the mother's borthers go far away to eat dirt. This is a description of a matrilineal group where children are permanently members of their mother's and her brothers' kin group. Their father used to make gardens but he is gone. That is, the father as an outsider to this matrilineal group has no continuing responsibility. Left on their own, the two sisters can provide themselves and their mother with easily gathered food, shrimp and crayfish.

The sisters meet Kapa, the Squirrel Spirit, a natural gatherer, who is transformed into a man with a tool. This tool is somewhat magical since the same word, *tipi,* is translated first as fish spear and later as fire maker. Squirrel produces the dry season by lowering the stream so that the sisters' gathering is made easy.

The mother is delighted to gain a son-in-law. However, she too would be a potential wife for Squirrel since in a matrilineal system she is of the same descent group as her daughters. The odd incident in which the mother is hit on the eyebrow by the branching manioc suggests that she should not enter her son-in-law's garden as long as she is neither his kin nor his wife.

The turning point of the story is the death of the young brother-in-law, Squirrel's *ania.* This death eliminates the possibility of Squirrel's children continuing the matrilineal tie with their mother's brother, and removes the son from his own house, which is essential for the structure of the matrilocal household.

The father then enters the picture and alienates Squirrel's kin. With the abolition of the matrilineal group Squirrel's kin are no longer the possible kin of his father-in-law, they are as Squirrel says, "My people, your affinals." Father and son-in-law are in different descent groups, and given the Sharanahua tendency to view their own social structure as consisting of only two descent groups, this eliminates any potential rivalry between the men for the same women. Father and daughter are in one descent group, mother and son-in-law are in the other. This is, of course, the ideal, the mythological structure, of a Sharanahua household. Once this pattern is reached, the mother can enter the garden that her son-in-law has cleared since she has become a member of Squirrel's descent group, a father's sister.

Hunting, however, brings in the problem of sex. The squirrel becomes a predator, a vampire bat, and his wife betrays him. "Your *rawi*," she says, "has been killed." Squirrel answers hypocritically, "Let us both weep." One's *rawi* is the cousin of one's wife, her potential or actual lover. It may be a man's brothers or the husband of one's wife's sister, but a *rawi* is a man who is in the same kinship category as oneself.

A man moves into a strange village in which his wife's kin protect her and expect their *raisi* to help provide for the household. He is aware that she has had love affairs with her cousins, and that they are still potentially her lovers or husbands. In contrast, her brothers, his *ania*, are not competitors. They are wife's brothers and potential friends or allies. At Marcos Forako calls Samuel *"ania"* because Forako's wife is a distant sister of Samuel's. But Samuel, who has ignored the incest taboo by marrying a "sister" is equally willing to redefine his wife's distant sister as a cousin. Samuel acts as Forako's *rawi*, but as long as Forako does not discover Samuel's love affair with his wife, they call each other *ania*, and they still help one another in burning gardens.

Rivalry between *rawi* is eliminated within the household itself by a man marrying sisters since two sons-in-law within the same house might compete. Outside the household, however, men are often rivals in their love affairs. This rivalry is concealed as all but righteous anger is hidden at Marcos, but the competition and hostility between men explodes at times when men take *bitishu* (manioc beer strengthened by fermentation with cane-sugar juice) or the rotgut *cachasa* that traders sell, both of which are innovations in Sharanahua life. Men start to drink at eight in the morning, by midday they are walking through the village, lurching against one another, occasionally falling off a house or cutting themselves. Young men show off their Spanish and imitate Peruvian bravado, speaking aggressively about honor, saying, "If anyone calls me a *caboclo*, I'll kill him." Tensions start to build as they get drunker and more argumentative, and Shamarua grabs his shotgun and shouts that he will kill Gustavo. Women rush to strip both houses of guns, machetes, and knives. Basta and Naikashu drag Gustavo away, trying to calm him. Baido and Zacharais try to talk Shamarua out of attack. Hosa, Shamarua's wife, looks terrified and seizes her three year old and hides in the bush behind the house. Gustavo, at his house, orders Ishamba to bring him water, and she refuses. He hits her with a flashlight, and she flees with her small children to her father's house.

Women occasionally have drinking parties, but they consume far less than the men. I have gone over to Basta's house when Bashkondi was asleep at noon in her hammock, Koyo and Shimiri were bleary eyed and dizzy. Women do not argue when they are drunk, though they rapidly pass out. There is no reason for strife between women at Marcos, aside from momentary personal quarrels, which are aired in gossip and tale bearing. They need only be good daughters, provocative women, antagonistic wives. Their subsistence labor is, perhaps, hard and repetitive, but they are never in a position to fail, and they are secure with their mothers and sisters.

Their security depends upon the extended and linked matrilocal households, the pattern of Marcos. Hunting and the distribution of meat still shape the basic structure of Marcos, though they are modified by the necessary cooperation of fishing and agriculture. However, the newer methods of fishing, begun only a few years ago, using harpoon and fishnets, may place a different emphasis on social life since it is possible for a small family unit or two men working together to count on a good catch. This may be the path of the future, if permanent settlement at Marcos exhausts the game and increases the Sharanahua's dependence upon fishing. One can sense this future path in the symbols of the hunter that appear in myth—the jaguar as hunter of Yawandi's myth is reduced to the vampire bat of Squirrel, in the myth that emphasizes agriculture.

The end of the story of Squirrel is unclear. It is left unstated whether Squirrel abandons his second wife so that she may return, as the jaguar's wife did, to her proper place, her father's house, or whether Squirrel leaves with his one wife and children to try unsuccessfully, as Samuel has done, to set up an independent household. Myths have their sources in the past, but the stories are transformed as Sharanahua reality, and their understanding of that reality, changes. In ten years, the story of Squirrel Spirit may present a different problem and a different solution, but today it begins to reveal the strains and contradictions that preoccupy the Sharanahua. The Squirrel myth seems to shuffle through the cards of social organization seeking solutions to the problems of organizing work, distribution, and consumption through rules of sex, generation, and descent. The *maloca* was one solution, Marcos is another, the future is still far off.

RITUAL

The Hallucinations of Social Solidarity

While strong drink is new to the Sharanahua and exposes emotions that are ordinarily prohibited and concealed, the drinking of *ayahuasca,* a powerful hallucinogenic drug, has long been an important ritual smoothly integrated into Sharanahua life. *Ayahusca* is the Spanish name for a vine that grows throughout the Amazon Basin. Several similar vines are grouped under this name or referred to as *yajé* or *caapi* and have been botanically identified as *Banisteriopsis caapi.* Sharanahua usually refer to the vine and the drink as *shori,* a Yaminahua word that has come to replace the older term, *ondi,* perhaps because Casha, who usually prepares the hallucinogenic, is Yaminahua. The word *rami* is often used as well to refer to the cooked brew, the hallucinations, or the songs that accompany the ritual. *Rami* means change or transformation and is expressive of the slowly shifting visual images, the hallucinations that fade gradually one into another.

Men following hunting trails or clearing land in a new place come upon the vine growing from its roots on the ground, climbing high up a nearby tree, its small flower far above, almost out of sight from the ground. A few men cut it down, chop it into two-foot lengths for easy carrying and bring it into the village. Other men who encounter the vine of *shori* tell Casha, the oldest shaman, where they have seen it.

Casha, the old shaman, cutting *shori*

Casha travels an hour or two, crossing the lake, walking toward the higher land away from the Purús, till he comes to a small natural clearing where he identifies the red of *shori* (*shori awu oshi*) and the stronger, bitter, black of *shori* (*shori awu fiso*), two varieties of the same plant. Casha has on occasion replanted *shori* in a garden near Marcos, but when it is used up he must travel to get it and to gather the leaves that must be brewed with it, *pishi kawa* and *batsi kawa*, two species of *Psychotria*.

About three in the afternoon Casha begins to pound the lengths of *shori*, then places them in a large pot with layers of leaves sandwiched in between. He pours in water and cooks it for a few hours, strains out the woody residue, and sets the liquid to cool. Casha cooks in front of Baiyakondi's house, where three logs are set up in a triangle to serve as seats for the men who will come later to take *shori*. Julio, Sharafo, and Onsika are learning to prepare the hallucinogenic, but they are still beginners. Baido and Ndaishiwaka, the two other shamans at Marcos, know how to prepare *shori* but rarely do so unless they need it for curing.

At eight in the evening men begin to stroll over to the small fire where Casha sits next to the large pot of *shori*. Two of the older men sit next to Casha: Baido, tall and thin, Ruapa, bald, a silver ornament hanging from his nose. On some evenings Baiyakondi joins this group. Younger men sit together, yet the logs are arranged so no man faces another. A line of men seated on one log face the banana trees past Ndaishiwaka's house; other men sit facing their backs or, on the third log, staring off into the scrubby second growth opposite Baiyakondi's clearing. Men stroll over, coming up the dark paths from their houses, usually walking alone toward the fire. Each man takes a cup or gourd bowl and dips into the pot, blows across the surface of the dark orange liquid that fills his cup, says a few words, "Let me see well," and then drinks down the bitter fluid.

For twenty minutes men chant quietly or gaze toward the distant black silhouette of the forest, lighting small pipes of Peruvian tobacco, picking a few stalks of an odorous plant (*Ocimum micranthum*), whose smell will protect them from bad visions. Most of the men hold long balsa poles, one end leaning on the ground, the other high above their heads as they sit. In the old days these were painted bright orange, but today they are plain.

The drug begins to take effect, and men get up, walk away from the fire, and lean on their sticks to vomit. They sway slightly and sit again as their vision fills with scrolls, like face-paint designs, brightly colored, and they chant a steady "he, he, he, he," while Casha begins to call the spirits of *shori* with his song. The scrolls grow larger, rope-like, snake-like, like the vine, changing, transforming, and each man tries to call the spirits, the visions, with his song.

One's ears and head are filled with the singing. The incessant rhythm pushes fear aside; circling shapes and colors shift like a kaleidescope. Someone sings of the pain of *shori*, the gut knotting and stretching, and snakes wind round and round. A cold wind rushing past marks the sensation of traveling, though the tropical night is still. The chanting increases, driving and effortful, several men take another bowlful of *shori*, and José sings, "the lake is coming, the spirits are coming"; Julio repeats and repeats the song of the banana tree, its dark leaves waving in the air; and Casha sings, *"ma dokwa,"* "it has arrived, the drunkeness of *shori* is here," and the spirits of *shori* come, beautiful women, dancing, with painted decorations and yellow feather hats. The singing continues more in unison, calmer now, and the spirits appear and reappear, changing shapes and sizes. On nights of bright moonlight, when chanting fills the air and men lean forward swaying with the long poles supporting them, eyes closed from the strength of the trance, the village is alive with spirits.

A few men come out of the trance, again light their pipes, stir the fire, and talk quietly to one another. They take another bowlful and continue their conversation, sometimes laughing softly and smiling until once again they feel the pain of *shori* and begin the chant, calling its drunkeness, calling the scrolls, the *kunu*, the *rami*, traveling to reach the spirits of *shori*. There are many songs and many different ways of singing the same song, but some version of the song of *shori* is usually sung:

At the edge of the lake a sprout of *shori* like a snake is growing,
Born in the lake, from the shore its snake-vine rises.
It is strong drunkenness, its strength comes strong so one feels it in the gut.
It is very strong, it has darkened our eyes, its colors come strong.
It hurts the gut, makes the flesh dark.
The pain of *shori*, the drunkenness comes.

The chanting continues throughout the night or until the pot of *shori* is empty and the spirits fade away. The men leave, each for his own hammock, to sleep a few hours until the morning noises of the village wake them. They say that if one has vomited the *shori* after each bowlful one is not drunk in the morning, and young men arise seemingly unaffected to fish or hunt, while old Baido does not take *shori* when he plans to work on his garden the following day.

During the two dry seasons I spent at Marcos, *shori* was taken two or three times a week; in the rainy season, only three or four times a month. It is possible that it was taken more often than I think since I was not specifically studying the *shori* ritual during the rainy season and may, therefore, have underestimated its frequency.

When I ask the men why they take *shori*, they reply that it is taken to seek the cause of illnesses and to learn or to know. Pushing the question further, a few men will answer that they want to know the world, to travel and see what lies beyond the Purús. Most men simply repeat that they want to know. Only two out of the thirty or more nights that I watched, was the ritual clearly aimed at curing the sick.

No one ever objected to my watching the ritual, and often I was asked to come and to tape the singing so that they could listen to it the next day. Men would ask me for cigarettes, and José and Sharafo often wandered over to where I sat, taking notes, on Baiyakondi's dark floor, to tell me about their visions, describing for a minute the beautiful young girls or the red snakes and then laughing and losing their speech as the drunkenness overwhelmed them, and they returned to their place on the log.

I had watched the sessions throughout one summer before finding the courage to take *shori* myself. An anthropologist and a biochemist who were working then at Zapote, the Culina village, visited me at Marcos and took *shori*. They told me that I would never understand what I was studying without participating and added that the experience was euphoric. It was toward the end of the field trip, and I decided that I would chance the women's disapproval, and one night asked to take it. A few men were doubtful, saying, I would weep and be frightened, that women did not know how to take *shori*. I told them I had watched many times and I would not be frightened, and finally Casha agreed.

Baiyakondi watched over me that first time, giving me a small bowlful, sitting beside me when I went deep into the trance. Finally he brought me out by holding the plant to my nose and asked me what I had seen. He laughed gently when I replied that I saw beautiful leaves and a tiny snake. One of the happier illusions of the *shori* trance is of understanding everything—the words of every chant even though they are metaphoric and the meaning of the ritual. I have taken *shori* five times and in reality the experience is often euphoric, occasionally terrifying. It made it possible to ask questions about the sensations and some of the visual images, which were common to everyone. These are the small scroll-like or bead-like images, which transform into ropes or snakes or vines and indicate that the drunkenness is beginning. These are considered of no importance. They are not the spirits, which must be called by someone who knows.

Not everyone can call the spirits. The younger men, still learning songs, maintain the rhythmic chant yet depend upon Casha's knowledge to bring their visions. Without singing, only snakes appear, and the first encounter with the snakes is terrifying to the young men. Later, after a year or so, as they continue to take *shori* and, like José, learn to know, they still see snakes, blue and red, coiled up in their stomachs and around their shoulders, but they find them beautiful. José's *rami* is good, he can call many spirits, while Nima still calls only a few. Baido and Ruapa, like Casha are experts—together calling and sharing visions of the spirits of the sky, of the world below ground, fish spirits and jaguar spirits, and the human-like spirits of *shori*.

They guide the young men, teasing them into chanting, blowing on their faces and stroking their foreheads if they appear too deep in a frightening trance, holding the sweet-smelling plant under their noses to bring them out.

The toxic or active elements contained in the cooked mixture of *shori* have been identified as harmine, tetrahydroharmine, and dimethyltryptamine. Research on the neurological effects of *shori* shows that it affects the sympathetic and parasympathetic nervous systems, producing such involuntary responses as yawning, salivating, vomiting, convulsing of the internal smooth muscles of lungs, stomach, and gut. (It has been suggested that the reason for women's abstinence from *ayahuasca* among most tropical forest groups, may be the danger of spontaneous abortion through its effect on the smooth muscle of the uterus.) The precise cause of the visual effects, the shifting colors and patterns, is not yet understood.

The small scrolls and rope-like images may be produced directly by the chemical acting on the nerves, but the visions of spirits that the Sharanahua seek are learned from the other men and from the beliefs that they share. Terror or euphoria also cannot be traced directly to the vine or a chemico-neurological reaction, but must be sought in the experiences that shape the ritual. Jaguars, snakes, and beautiful women cannot be found in a vegetable substance or located at a nerve ending. They are symbolic images learned as language is learned through interaction and communication with those who have them, stored as perceptions, and triggered by the drunkenness, the singing, the ritual of *shori*.

The young men must learn to shape the visual illusions and the physiological sensations into the mold and form of the spirits. This is what the Sharanahua mean when they say that José "knows" whereas Nima is just beginning to understand. At first, the context in which this was said led me to believe that José had learned many chants while Nima knew only one. When I asked my informants if this was what they meant, they agreed.

Further thought, however, showed that their idea of learning a *shori* song was not simply a matter of learning the words and melody. Sharanahua learn other songs with great facility. Their memory for words and melodies is excellent, and the songs of *shori* are not especially complex. The knowing that takes several years to master is to see the spirits that Casha and the experienced men call and, by learning the songs, to share the hallucinations. Men sing of what they see and their singing calls the visions.

This process is not essentially different from the everyday experience in which, as someone describes a scene or an object, the listener pictures it in his mind. Hallucinations seem more vivid and more real, less apparently controllable, yet ordinary words can also create intense but predictable emotional states and behavior, and thoughts and images appear in one's mind spontaneously in the presence of a good listener. The magical quality of hallucinations, of course, is that they appear outside the creating mind, projected onto the outside world of apparent reality. Such symbols can frighten or enchant, seduce or torture the beholder with his own meanings, his own bodily sensations.

When Sharanahua first take *shori* they are frightened. The snakes that encircle them are only slowly transformed, after months of taking part in the ritual, into beautiful images. This transformation of terror to euphoria is another kind of learning, and this learning, I believe, is a significant part of the ritual. The terror of *shori* for a Sharanahua is the terror of strangers, the very men with whom one takes *shori*. For most young men these are not his kinsmen, but *yura futsa* in whose village or household he has found a wife. As the young men continue to take part, their fears fade, the snakes are beautiful, and they begin to learn to call the spirits and "to know."

Several people told me about the Peruvian who took *shori* with them. As the drug began to take effect he started to scream and ran toward the river. Fearing that he would jump into the river or stumble on the dark path, several men ran after him.

He continued to run until he was at the water, and he screamed as they held him back. He told them later he had seen *indios bravos,* "wild Indians," threatening to kill him with their spears and bows and arrows, and that he thought when they followed him that they were chasing him to kill him. *Shori* is a powerful drug, and the Peruvian could not control his real fear of Indians, which is the obverse of the contempt that openly characterizes the relationship between Peruvians and Indians. His own fears were, perhaps, further triggered by the covert hostility of the men with whom he took *shori.*

The terrors of *shori* are real. They lie below the surface of everyday life to appear before the frightened eyes of the young men. The competition between kinsmen refracted onto the hostility to *yura futsa* is symbolized in the fearsome snakes. Through the recurring ritual experiences these strangers are transformed into friendly visions; as in the myth of *shori* the threatening sting ray is transformed into *ishki,* the harmless catfish.

"I will tell you about Snake-Spirit," Basta began:

A man built a hunting blind next to the shore of the lake, and one day as he was concealed there he saw a tapir spirit carrying genipa on its back. As the man watched, the tapir threw the genipa fruits one after another into the lake. The water began to splash, and rising from the water was Snake-Spirit, Snake-Woman. She was beautiful, with long hair, and having received the genipa, she came to the tapir, and the man watched as the tapir stood over her and copulated with her. The man became excited as he watched the tapir copulate with her, and he wanted to do the same. Then Snake-Woman returned, splashing, to the deep water, and the tapir left, and the man ran to gather genipa, lots of it.

He had heard Snake-Woman ask the tapir how soon he would return and had heard the answer, so in that number of days he went to the lake and, just like the tapir, threw the genipa fruits, one after another into the water. He hid himself and watched as Snake-Woman, splashing, appeared. She searched around and said, "Where are you?" And as she searched the man grabbed her around her ribs.

Then as the man listened to her snake speech he was frightened, but she coiled around him and pulled him toward the lake. He grabbed her and now she changed and was beautiful, then she became huge, up to the sky. She kept changing and transforming until she became his size. Now he saw her lovely paint and he desired her. Now they stood together, and she said, "Who are you? You are afraid, but I want to be with you."

"You don't have a husband?" he asked.

"No, I don't."

Then they copulated over and over, like the tapir, yes, in that way they copulated. "Let's go," she said, "I have no husband." She gathered leaves and rubbed and squeezed them into his eyes. Then he could see deep in the lake a huge house. As they were going to the house, they encountered her people moving within the deep. He saw all kinds of fish—*boca chica* came, sting ray threatened him with his tail, *tunofo,* holding his throwing spear, asked, "What are you doing, *chai* [cousin of the same sex]?" He saw the evil alligator with his spear. Underwater spirits, hairless underwater spirits. Then he saw his father-in-law, an old man with frightening paint. His mother-in-law was the same. Down there the man and Snake-Woman kept copulating.

The old father-in-law was taking *shori,* lots of them were taking it. "I want to take it with you," the man said to his wife.

"You must never take it," she said. "My father taught me to take it, but you must not."

But, despite her words, he took it. He took *shori,* and he got drunk on *shori.* And then he saw! His father-in-law's frightening paint, he was a huge snake! His wife drunkenly clinging to him was a snake! "The snake wants to eat me!" he screamed.

"A snake is not eating you," she said.

His father-in-law blew on him. His wife blew on him. "Human," she said, "I told you not to, but you took *shori.* I will not eat you. I am holding you." She kept blowing on him until he was no longer drunk.

Now her people were angry at him for what he had said, but he saw Ishki in his small house, making a feather hat. "Ishki, Ishki, *chai isht*a [dear, little cousin], what are you doing?

"I'm making my feather hat, *chai*," said Ishki. "Your many children and your wife are sad and weeping for you, *chai.*"

The underwater spirits were swimming back and forth, looking for him, and Ishki said, "I'll take you back, dear *chai.* Hold onto my hair. We'll go to your home."

The underwater spirits kept threatening and asking Ishki what he was doing and what his *chai* was saying. But Ishki said nothing and went splashing away with the man holding onto his hair. Ishki left the man standing by the lake and swam away, pursued by the fish spirits grabbing at him. He swam and swam, Ishki, dear *chai*, until he came to his house, and there he hid with all his children.

"Thus, Snake-Spirit, my father told me long ago, and I listened."

Many features of this story are uniquely Sharanahua, although the myth is made up of elements that occur in other people's myths. The lake is *shori,* and the snake is the bridge, the vine that leads men into trance. Snake-Woman is the foreign seductress who leads men into marriage, in which, as they move to their affinals' home, they find those frightening snakes, their *raisi,* and all their wife's kin, *yura futsa,* the underwater spirits who threaten them.

As Snake-Woman is the bridge into the lake, so Ishki is the bridge out, the friendly brother-in-law, the *chai* transformed. Snake-Woman has long hair and emerges splashing, just as Ishki is a fish with hair and splashes away with the hero. In the *shori* trance the danger of women is momentarily transformed into the aid of a man, but Ishki, like the hero, returns isolated to his home.

The terrors of *shori* are childhood terrors, and the experience of the trance is one of helplessness. Like an infant, one is in the control of *shori* and the spirits. By giving up the cultural role of adulthood, as the man gives up being a hunter to imitate the tapir, one again experiences desires long buried for freely given satisfaction, sex without antagonism, friendship without rivalry.

In the trance the voices chanting overwhelm the terror. The intense pleasure of *shori* lies in these moments of connection, which evoke, perhaps, desires and experiences dimly remembered. This is the need and this is what pushes men to take *shori,* but the myth also states the cultural premise, the waking restrictions of Sharanahua life. To openly desire is to be like an animal and to be led into danger. The truth is that people are dangerous and friendship an illusion, and in the real world one must hide one's childishness, like Ishki, and fulfill one's cultural role.

Boys hunt and fish together, leaving their households most of the day, by the time they are about ten. They play, but some of their expeditions are more serious since any small bird or lizard will be lunch, and they are not always offered food at midday in their own households. A few adolescent boys, like Coshamba's son, early join the households of their father's sister as future husbands to their young cousins, but this is no sure guarantee of their future status. For most boys the companionship of their youth falls away as they search for wives in other villages, hunt by themselves, and live with foreign women surrounded by foreigners. It is these young men for the most part who join their elders in the village in the ritual of *shori,* seeking in the visions of the hallucinogenic drug, the sense of commonality and belonging that is an elusive shadow at Marcos.

Watching the *shori* sessions week after week, I have seen the old men, Baido, Casha, Ruapa, and sometimes Baiyakondi, sit together, chant, and hallucinate. Baido is easily chilled by the *batsi kawa* and frequently passes his hand over the fire and then across his forehead. He asks Casha to blow over his face, and Casha strokes Baido's head expertly to help remove the pain of *shori* or to bring Baido out of the trance. Ruapa is an Amahuaca, recently married, despite his age, and a man who "knows," and he too sits at ease with the others. Baiyakondi has often been sick during the past three years and, therefore, takes *shori* less frequently. But he too sits at ease, taking *shori* with the other old men.

These four old men, all perhaps in their sixties, spend little time together in the daytime, even though Casha at times stays in Baiyakondi's house, where he is married to Yaka, Baiyakondi's twelve-year-old granddaughter. They eat in their own households alone, or with their wives and children. It is an unusual sight to see any of them in conversation or activity together outside of the *shori* ritual.

The same is true of the younger men, who also appear less related during the ritual, more individualistic in the visions they describe and the chants they sing. At times Nima and Onsika joke together during a sober interval and chant in unison, while Tohukai sings loudly and aggressively, standing, swaying with his hands tightly clasped on the long pole. Bito, a Mastinahua, married into Marcos only a year, chants a little and then stops, never appears drunk, and always leaves early.

There are only four men at Marcos who do not take part in the ritual. Basta and Zacharais used to take the drug but have given it up for the last few years and say that they have too much work to do. They say that if they take *shori* they find it hard to get up early in the morning for hunting or making gardens. They are the two most important men at Marcos, practical and organized, directing large households. It is difficult to know just what has affected them. Perhaps, it is because Marcos is in a sense their village, and they are in the prime of life, not yet old like Baiyakondi, Baido, and Casha, no longer insecure like the younger men or strange to the village like Ruapa. In addition, they and their households are the most friendly to the missionaries. While the missionaries have no leverage to openly oppose *shori*, their low opinion of the drug and the ritual is obvious.

Their sons, Gustavo and Samuel, are the other two men. Gustavo is contemptuous of the ritual. He says that *shori* is bad but *cachasa* is fine. Samuel is terrified of the drug. He took it for more than a year and continually experienced the hallucinations as frightening. The last time he took it he saw a huge snake, soldiers, and a man like the *guardia civil* (a Peruvian policeman)—hairless with boots and cartridges across his chest. It is tempting to argue that as men who have not had to live matrilocally, Gustavo and Samuel are not sufficiently motivated by isolation to overcome their fear of strangers. Yet, it is not that simple, Shamarua also lives patrilocally, and he takes *shori*. He is isolated in the sense that his father's household, Baido's, has few kin in the world, and, in fact, Shamarua takes *shori* less frequently than most of the other men.

Ndaishiwakà now takes *shori* only when he is curing since he considers it dangerous to his eyes. He is losing the sight of one eye, and he says that the morning sun is painful after he takes *shori*.

Women do not take *shori* at Marcos, with the exception that when Yawandi's first husband died ten years ago, she took some with Chatafundia, searching for the cause of his death. The contradictions of adulthood are more striking for men than for women at Marcos. Women's loyalty to their kin is not crossed with competition. They have neither the threat nor the opportunity of confronting strangers to challenge their steady dependence upon kin or to reawaken past memories of childhood pleasures with other people with whom they had no obligations or expectations beyond companionship.

When I first met Shomoiya she was perhaps two or three years old, still the youngest of Samuel's household, curious, affectionate, spontaneous. The next year she tagged after her older sister, but ran back to her mother, Ifama, now caring for the newest infant, often angry and sorrowing that her mother, busy with the baby, pushed away her attempts to hang onto her. Teasing boys made her angry, although she was a flirtatious little girl. At five, Shomoiya spends a few minutes holding her baby brother in the baby sling which drapes her shoulders and spends most of the day with Koyone, her cousin, cooking small pieces of manioc in a tiny pot, putting their rag dolls—a folded cloth —to sleep. Her conversation is the usual gossip of every woman, and she masterfully flirts with and rebuffs the boys and men who call her bimbiki, "cousin." Her life is set now in the pattern of her future. Secure, if dull and frustrating, Shomoiya's life will keep her with her parents and sisters, working a bit more, playing somewhat less, flirtations changing to love affairs; the woman she is to become is already formed and, barring misfortune, nothing will shatter the smooth confines of her life.

Sharanahua men say that women do not know how to take shori and that women prefer to sleep. The women tell me that they do not like it. Despite the apparent casualness of these statements, there is a strong disapproval of women taking part in the ritual. No woman at Marcos has ever asked or wanted to listen to what the experience is like. There is no stronger moral condemnation than to actively ignore an act of which one disapproves. Bashkondi and Yawandi have questioned me in detail on every other area of my life that lies within their comprehension. Even when we worked on transcribing the myth of

Snake-Spirit, and they told me that I was like Snake-Woman, they made no mention of *shori,* only referring to the odd facts that I was brave to travel alone and I smoked. Yet the connection was there, though unmentioned, and as we continued working on this myth Yawandi added that Tundo was a Snake-Woman. Tundo has never borne children although she helped raise Baiyakondi's children after their mother died. She and Baiyakondi are affectionate and close to one another in a way that is rare at Marcos. And further, she comes from a village far away, where the women take *shori,* and she "knows."

Several people had told me that Tundo knew how to take *shori* and that her songs were good. I asked her to sing so that I could tape it, and she replied that she could only sing if she took *shori.* She agreed to take it if her husband were taking it and if he would bring it to her. Although she had told me that in her own village, the women used to take it with the men, she stayed in her hammock in the house, while the men sat as usual in front of Baiyakondi's house.

She chanted in a sort of counterpoint to the men's singing. They would pause, and she would sing, and there was a bantering rivalry between Tundo and the men which brought to my mind thoughts of football games, and I had an auditory hallucination of a brass band. Although none of the men had ever taken *shori* with a woman singing, they responded as if they had always sung against just such a counterpoint. While the pattern of the chants was different that night, the dynamics of the ritual were the same: a feeling of communality between the men achieved through their shared desire and antagonism toward women. There is no other basis for male solidarity at Marcos, no loyalty overriding the divisions between descent groups, no unity to compensate for the competition between brothers.

The symbolism of some songs is an evocation of sexual images as the chant reverberates with a driving rhythm like sex. I asked Ndaishiwaka once if men felt desire when they took *shori*. He replied that some did, listing them, and added that they usually had sexual intercourse afterward with their wives. He said that taking *shori* was like sex, but not in the sense that everyone actually became desirous.

Two adolescent boys, Shandi and Dikandi, sometimes take *shori* with the men. They take only a little and joke and laugh, pointing at the hole in Casha's worn pants that exposes his penis, imitating for a moment the men's chants and then giggling and rolling on the ground. Usually they leave early without getting drunk. Shandi took it one night when I was there and, as I came partially out of the *shori* trance, I realized that Shandi was lying on the ground, watching me and masturbating. Masturbation is not openly engaged in at Marcos. Again, as in the case of incest, Shandi could not maintain the social rules and forced into the open one of the underlying sensations that is transformed in the *shori* ritual.

Learning to take *shori* is learning to share the visions, the spirits, of the others around you. When this occurs one can chant the songs that describe them and can try with the other men to reach the drunkenness of *shori* together. This unison does not occur every night that *shori* is taken, but often one hears the break in the rhythm as the driving chant shifts to the climactic song that says it has arrived, the drunkenness of *shori*, and Casha sings of *yura futsa* women, Julio of Culina women, and José of Mastinahua. Old men see the women of *shori* dressed in short woven skirts, with monkey-teeth bracelets on arms and legs, beautiful paint on their bodies and faces, and feather hats for dancing. Young men see women with cotton dresses, beaded necklaces and arm bands, and painted faces.

In back of Baiyakondi's house, somewhat concealed from sight by bushes of *pooikama* for poisoning fish, is a small planting of cacti, called *chai*. (There is no apparent connection between this word and the homonym that means "cousin.") It is said to be stronger even than black *shori* with which it is occasionally cooked. One night when Baiyakondi and Ruskufunda took *chai* they saw the thorns of the cactus. Rushkufunda was frightened and saw nothing more, but Baiyakondi saw the people of *chai*, many beautiful ocelots, a black dog, and Peruvians in a launch with snakes around their necks. Baido during the same night saw fish, then a huge wooden thing, lots of men with red face paint, lots of girls and women with one eye.

At times Casha sings the song of the launch and brings visions of Peruvian spirits, traveling up the Purús in a large boat filled with things: pots and beads, shells, guns, tobacco, cloth, suitcases, and *cachasa*. Baido with a look of ecstasy says out loud, though deep in the trance, "twenty thousand *soles*," and returns to the chant. I once asked Tohukai, after he had described his hallucinations of the Peruvian launch arriving at Marcos, whether he had seen them giving their things away. He answered that of course they had not—Peruvians never give things away. While Casha sang, Nima saw lots of people and huge things with motors, large snakes and men marching. Tararai saw lots of Peruvians, cows, huge snakes, and women. Casha saw lots of people coming, some Peruvians with snakes around them, a huge machine, and women with red paint, necklaces, and feathered hats.

In the ritual men share their visions and desires in the hours of dark blue nights lit by stars. A single fire warms them as the chanting and the transformations of *shori* hold them closely together. Like their shadows cast by moonlight on the cleared ground, the visions, the chanting, the closeness vanish in the reality of day. The ritual occurs and reoccurs, over and over, creating an hallucination of social unity.

8

SHAMAN

Visions and Cures

I had been at Marcos only a few months when Basta and Gustavo appeared at my house one afternoon and angrily told me to stop giving medicine to the strangers who came to Marcos. "They come here sick, and when they are well they leave and do no work," said Basta.

"The medicines you have are for us," said Gustavo. "Let them die," and he laughed.

We argued for some time back and forth, and I pointed out that Basta himself had asked me for medicine for his kin from Boca de Curanja. That, he said, was fine, but I must not waste medicine on *yura futsa*. I told him I had plenty of pills, enough to give to strangers. At that both men relaxed, and Basta said, "That's fine, give them pills, just don't cure them."

This rejoinder left me uneasy since it implied that I could cure when I wanted to and that whenever I gave pills rather than penicillin injections, people assumed I was not really trying to cure them. I tended to avoid giving injections whenever possible, in part because sterilization was always doubtful, in part because I dislike giving injections. I preferred, if an antibiotic seemed necessary, to use tetracyclin capsules. While penicillin was incredibly effective in curing some illnesses, there were many ailments for which it was totally useless. Yet the belief in the magical powers of injections, one which is shared by many Peruvians, led Basta and others to exert sufficient social pressure to enforce my compliance many times.

Marcos is fortunately free of the deadly tropical forest disease, yellow fever, and other European imported diseases such as malaria and tuberculosis have not yet made real inroads. Physically, the Sharanahua appear to have great stamina and strength, and I have watched Casha, who must be past sixty, rapidly climb to reach the fruit of a papaya tree and Yawanini, the same age, carry a load of wood that I was unable to lift. The level of parasite infection in this sparsely populated region appears to be nowhere near the heights of more "civilized" jungle areas, such as the regions near large towns such as Pucallpa and Iquitos, but no one at Marcos is free of amoeba and other intestinal parasites, and these are the causes of most strange aches of stomach and liver.

Minor wounds and ailments are generally cared for by the application of herbs and leaves. Stomach pains and diarrheas are often handled by changing the diet. When the illness appears more serious, one of the men of the household will blow smoke over the patient's body, rubbing the ailment out. When more specialized knowledge is needed, Basta is often consulted. He is not a shaman, but he is expert at the selection and preparation of herbal remedies, handling a range of ailments from severe toothaches to serious wounds.

The Sharanahua have learned about penicillin from Dominican and American missionaries, and they consider it a powerful medicine, but it cannot attack the spirits that seek to kill, that afflict the ailing person so that he "wants to die." A belief in spirits, particularly dangerous and menacing spirits, is common throughout the tropical forest. No child growing up at Marcos, seeing the marks where spirits have sucked blood, hearing the wails of women whose husbands have not returned from the forest by nightfall, watching people jump with terror as a sudden bolt of thunder announces the waking of angry,

murderous spirits, can escape this belief system. The Sharanahua tread warily in the forest that lies beyond their clearings
and avoid the friendly appearing stranger outside of their village.
As a belief in sin may be used to guide behavior and explain
misfortune, so for the Sharanahua does the belief in spirits
explain illnesses that do not respond to practical treatment.

One need only fear the spirit of one's kin for the few
weeks while it is still angry at leaving this life and lingers near
the house, trying to kill a kinsman to accompany it. A few
weeks after death, a spirit flies back to the land of its birth where
it resides forever or, according to some Sharanahua, it eventually leaves its birthplace for a land in the sky. There is a small
bird called *yoshi*, "spirit," that has a strange cry and flies high,
which is said to be such a spirit returning to its land. The
Sharanahua say one should burn all of the property of the
dead, including the house, so the spirit will not desire to stay.

Other spirits, those of foreign people, animals, fish, or rainbows, are always menacing. They lie in wait, hungering for
human blood, human fat, human meat. Even a brave man
starts at an inexplicable noise at night and avoids entering
the forest, preferring, if he must be away from Marcos, to
stay at a strange village or to build a *tambo*, a makeshift shelter
on the beach along the river. Nonetheless, one may be attacked.
Chochoya showed me the bruise where a spirit had begun to
eat him as he slept on the beach, and Samuel showed the
mark on his arm of a spirit's bite when he returned from
Zapote. Every animal, every fish, and every person has a spirit,
and there are strange, foreign, human-shaped spirits who live in
the forest.

"I shall tell you an old story about spirits":

A man had killed a paca, but when he went to find it only
the blood remained, and he wondered who had taken the
paca from him. As he walked through the forest he came

to a clearing where he saw someone cooking meat and gulping it down.

"Did you take my paca," he asked.

"Yes, chai [cousin], come on over, chai. Ai cho! My chai has arrived," said the spirit, and he leaned back. The man was very angry as he watched the spirit fan the fire. "Let's eat, chai," said the spirit, "I will serve you."

The man wanted his paca, and the spirit was eating its liver, so the man said, "Chai, turn around, look over there." The spirit turned and looked, and the man lifted the pot of water from the fire and dumped it over the spirit.

"Ari! Ari! Chai! Chai! It hurts!" and the spirit fell over.

The man was frightened but took the meat from the spirit's plate and put the rest of the paca meat in his basket.

"Chai, chai, give me back the paca!" screamed the spirit.

"Drop dead!" said the man.

Later the man's mother's brother came, and the man told him how he had finished off the spirit. The two men continued through the forest and came to a clearing where spirits were dancing. The evil spirit said, "Come chai, let's dance."

The man was angry and suddenly shot an arrow at the spirit's head, but it didn't kill it. The spirit said, "Chai, you're cutting my hair." The spirit wanted to grab the man and said, "Come here."

The man shot another arrow, and it grazed the spirit's face. "Stop it, chai," said the spirit, "the shave hurts."

The man grabbed the spirit's hair and pulled it hard. "Chai, chai, it hurts, it hurts! Let go, chai." The man ran away but the spirit was angry.

Some time went by and the man had a child so he

went to the forest to get genipa. The spirit came along looking for him and asked, "What are you getting, *chai?*"

"I want to get genipa for my child."

"There's some over there, *chai*, it's very near. Let's go get it."

They kept going and going. The man kept asking where it was, and the spirit kept saying it was near, and they walked until evening when they came to a genipa tree. The spirit said, "Go, get it. I'll wait for you down here."

The man climbed up, and then many spirits came, the spirit's kin came. The man was afraid, and he made himself a big stick, a club, and he fled further up the tree. The spirits started climbing after him, and he heard them say, "I will eat that bad one." They wanted to eat his liver with manioc.

The man was sitting up high on a branch, and the spirit kept climbing, but not the way people climb. The spirit climbed ass first, and, as each spirit came near, "tsosh!" the man stabbed it in the ass, and it fell. They kept coming, hungering for his liver, to cook it with manioc, and the man kept hitting them.

Then the spirits went to get axes. They were made of the shoulder blades of deer and armadillo, the shoulder bones of game animals. They chopped and chopped and slowly the genipa tree fell down. The man dropped his stick and, as the tree crashed, he fled into an armadillo hole. The spirits pushed a rope down the hole, but he went further in so they could not find him. From the hole the man saw the spirits chasing a deer. The deer said nothing, but it fled. The man started to pull himself out of the hole, but as he got his head out a spirit grabbed him by the throat. The spirits painted themselves with genipa and ate him.

After a while the man's older brother came looking for

him and went to the big tree near where his brother had been, but the spirits were lying in wait. As the man began to climb, they rushed after, grabbing at him. He fled to another tree where there was a wild turkey's nest. There were lots of game and fruit which he ate. He woke early in the morning, not knowing the spirits were waiting outside, and as he left they grabbed him, holding his mouth so he could not yell. The tree was swaying back and forth. It crashed and a flock of wild turkeys flew out, eating fruit and whistling. The spirits stopped to shoot the birds, and the man saw a young bird drop a wrist bone! a foot bone! from which the meat had been eaten.

"What evil spirit ate my brother!" The spirits went away, but the man never found his younger brother.

The story makes the point several times that man hunting game is hunted by spirits. The first part of the story about the man who gets the better of the spirit who has eaten his paca serves as an explanation for the spirit's attack on the man when he is only looking for genipa. It also underlines the spirit's hunger for livers, animal or human. The spirits succeed in getting him out of the tree, forcing him to hide like an armadillo, by cutting the tree down with an axe made of the bones of game animals. His brother in turn hides in a bird's nest and is almost taken after eating game. In another version of this story, the brother is also eaten.

The similarity between animal and human physiology is obvious to every child at Marcos, and language makes no distinction between the body, flesh, bones, and internal organs of animals and humans. The myth of the origin of peccaries expresses this similarity by showing how peccaries were once human. In another myth a man kills a paca, and the paca's wife, sad and angry, visits the man's wife to take revenge. "Cousin," says the paca-wife to the woman, "Your husband has killed my husband," and the paca-wife starts to attack the woman and her children. No Sharanahua hunts for pleasure or kills more game than he can carry. While the necessary preoccupation with procuring food makes sentimental feeling about animal life impossible or unbearable, the perceived likeness between men and animals leads readily to the equation that as man hunts animals so will he be hunted by spirits; as humans cut up game, relishing the fat, the liver, the good meat, so do the spirits.

The ubiquity of spirits and the impossibility of killing them seem to personify a feeling of helplessness in the face of an environment so beautiful and so cruel. On the river or working on a garden the sun hurts, "It is eating," the Sharanahua say, and heads ache for the rest of the day. The incessant gnats feed all day, and, as one lies in a hammock, someone leans over and slaps hard and says, "sandfly," and a black fly, fat with human blood, falls dead. Sundown is a moment of relief which even a hundred mosquitoes cannot mar.

In cold spells one shivers and wakes every two hours at night to get a new plateful of coals to warm the *mosquitero*. Everyone coughs and gets colds and sleeps poorly, and a day later an onslaught of vomiting and diarrhea sets children weeping and parents worrying. Tiny cuts on bare feet become torturous to walk on in the cold. In the rainy season men's feet and children's bodies break out in pussy sores, and the infection spreads to raise fevers and painful swelling of the lymph glands, which, accurately, is considered a dangerous sign. Nothing is ever dry for more than a few hours, people complain of old-age bone aches, stiff fingers, sore throats, conjunctivitis, and fever.

In the forest someone shouts to warn of an *isula,* the huge stinging ants that make one drunk with pain, and, reaching for a handhold on a tree, one must avoid a swarm of red fire ants. Returning, one looks for ticks, huge tapir ticks, gray and voracious, or worse, the almost invisible tiny red ticks that burrow into the skin and hurt for a week. The women dig the egg sacs of chiggers out of toes skillfully so that the sac does not break to leave a budding worm to swell the foot, and they break each and every tiny egg with a needle so that it does not lie in wait for another bare foot. An infected gnat drops a worm's egg into the leg while sucking blood, and two weeks later the pain of the worm turning in the leg is excruciating, and it must be removed by daubing an old, foul, drop of tobacco juice on the skin and slowly winding the worm out on a stick. Women and girls pick lice out of men's hair and their own, break them in their teeth and eat them. When faced by a new animal or insect I learned to ask both, "Do we eat it?" and "Does it eat us?" One cannot escape the feeling that one is hunted as well as hunter in the forest, prey as well as predator.

Aches and fevers, snake bite and diarrhea, any sickness may be curable with forest leaves, herbs, or penicillin injections, but if someone "wants to die," *na pai,* only a shaman can save him by finding the spirit that has attacked him and controlling it. The ailing person lies within his *mosquitero,* usually on the floor, and refuses to eat. Everyone says, "He wants to die," and the women enter the *mosquitero,* hold him in their arms, wailing and chanting over and over, "My child is dying, my child is dying." Small children, members of the household or descent group, are taken into the stifling *mosquitero* and sit at the edge, crying with fear and confusion.

A shaman is called, at times all three shamans are called, and he asks the sick man about his symptoms and his dreams. If he has not dreamed, a curing song is chosen on the basis of his symptoms alone. Thus, when Samuel drunkenly cut deep into his foot with a machete and the blood kept flowing out and he wanted to die, the shaman sang of the machete, and the wound healed. If *shori* is not easily available, the shamans may begin curing without taking it, basing his songs on his patient's dream as Ndaishiwaka did when his wife, Chatafundia, still sick after giving birth with great difficulty, told him she had dreamed of a large snake and of human spirits eating her. He sang of the snake and the human spirits. Since she was still sick the following day, Ndaishiwaka and Casha cooked *shori* in order to find and control the spirits that were causing her to die. Casha was able to see in the vision that *shori* brought, that a large snake was encircling Chatafundia, and as he sang, he unwound the snake from her body, and she began to recover.

Ndaishiwaka discussed twenty-seven cases he could remember treating within the recent past. Only with Chatafundia was he unable to sing her free from the imperiling spirits. The shamans take *shori* with the other men. As they chant the shaman sings a curing song and slowly a vision appears of the image from the sick man's dream, the spirit that is causing his death. The shaman describes his visions vividly as they unfold before his eyes.

The shaman's sister-in-law, Tomuha, was vomiting, her liver hurt, and she strongly wanted to die. Her father-in-law went to bring Ndaishiwaka, who was working away from the village at the time. The next morning he arrived at the village. He asked Tomuha what she had dreamed, and she described seeing a high bank of the river. In her dream she climbed up and sat there alone. Then the shaman sang about a high bank on the river. Tomuha was slightly better the next day but still very ill, so he went to get *shori,* cooked it, and drank it that night. He saw the high bank and Tomuha sitting alone. Then a Culina came near her and said, "You will die, Tomuha," and threw a magical substance into her so that she vomited and cried. "But I am there," said the shaman, "and I am shaking my spear, and the Culina is frightened and runs away. And you will not die, Tomuha." Then Ndaishiwaka sang about *dori,* the magical substance. He saw Tomuha coming up the river, alone in a canoe, and Tomuha was cured.

Yopira, a woman of about thirty, is Baido's wife. Her stomach had ached for days, and she slept and slept. Baido and Casha had tried to cure her without success. Baido called Ndaishiwaka and the three shamans took *shori,* but still Baido and Casha could not cure her. Yopira had dreamed of a capybara, and when Ndaishiwaka took *shori*, he saw the capybara going around Yopira, clawing her back and eating her. Ndaishiwaka told Yopira to make a big fire to burn the capybara, and the capybara died. He told Yopira and Baido to eat the capybara, which they did even though they were unable to see it. Then Ndaishiwaka saw a spirit, a man who looked like a monkey, taking *shori*. Yopira was cured. During this cure, Ndaishiwaka sang for two days, taking *shori* both nights. In addition to the capybara, which he felt was the significant vision and song, he had seen and sung of the land turtle and a snake.

Chicolopez, a man of about fifty-five, is the shaman's father's brother. Ndaishiwaka was called to the village where Chicolopez was living. He had a bad headache and shook all over. The Dominican priest had come from Esperanza to give him pills and injections of penicillin, but Chicolopez was still very sick. He had dreamed of a huge monkey, like a howler monkey, but very large. A male with painted designs on its forehead, white hands and white feet. Ndaishiwaka took *shori* and sang of the howler monkey, then he saw it, a huge one. It was eating fruit in the trees. The monkey grabbed Chicolopez, but the shaman told it to leave him alone, and it ran away. The next night the shaman saw a different kind of monkey. It was black and white, and it was eating people. He saw lots of people and lots of monkeys eating them. The monkeys wanted to eat Chicolopez. A huge one was coming, so the shaman took a bow and arrow and hit it. The monkeys yelled and ran away in all directions. The shaman told Chicolopez, "You dreamed of these monkeys, now I see them. I have hit them with my bow, and they are running away." The third night Chicolopez dreamed of a peccary. The shaman saw a huge peccary coming toward Chicolopez, biting him. Ndaishiwaka shot the peccary with his shotgun. It did not die, but it ran away. Then Chicolopez began to eat a little, and his shaking lessened. On the fourth night Ndaishiwaka sang about *mama,* the traditional corn drink. The next morning he gave some to Chicolopez, and he was well.

Although it is usual to have more than one shaman take part in a cure, Ndaishiwaka usually claimed the credit for success. "I alone cured him," he would say. When his father, Baiyakondi, was vomiting, Ndaishiwaka sang of watermelons and had a vision of many watermelons on the beach. His father was eating them, and he told him to stop. In the vision Baiyakondi stops and is cured. The other shaman, Baido, saw a huge fish, and though the fish went away, Baiyakondi was not cured. Unfortunately, Ndaishiwaka did not tell me the dream in this case, but it seems likely that the elements in the dream were differently used by the two shamans. It also appears likely that had my informant been Baido, the story might have been different.

In several cases themes derived from Peruvian culture appear. Ruatay, a girl of about eleven, had been sick at a time when I was working at Marcos. She had what appeared to be grippe and a bad cough with extremely high fever, and I was unsuccessful in treating her with a broad-spectrum antibiotic. Ruatay had dreamed of an airplane and the sun hurting her. Ndaishiwaka sang of the plane and he saw Ruatay flying on it. As he continued to sing the plane vanished and Ruatay was cured.

One of the shaman's younger brothers, Tohukai, had been sick with grippe for six days. He had a high fever and was coughing blood. Ndaishiwaka called Felisario from the village of Curanja, and they took *shori*. Ndaishiwaka saw an accordion grabbing Tohukai around the chest. He sang of the accordion, and it went away. Felisario saw an harmonica, which also disappeared as he continued to sing, and Tohukai was a little better. Then Ndaishiwaka saw a bead necklace, beads of white, red, and black such as the Peruvian traders sell, which was strangling Tohukai. He sang about the necklace; it went away and Tohukai got better. The Peruvian objects as well as the animals, the Culina, and the watermelon are all part of the world of the spirits.

When the patient starts to improve, the shaman usually retires to his own house, drinks a small amount of *shori* from a special small clay pot, and sings into the pot, which gives a strange vibrating sound to the singing. The next morning the shaman offers his patient a drink of *mama* from this pot. Usually a patient takes nothing but this corn drink and boiled banana drink for a day. Then he eats fish and, when fully recovered, returns to his normal diet.

The shaman who looks for the cause of illness in the visions of *shori* and cures by singing over his patient makes use of the kind of communication that occurs in the *shori* ritual. In part the shaman consciously utilizes and manipulates the internal states expressed in images, conscious in the way and at the level that poets or musicians manipulate verbal imagery or sound to produce emotional affects in the experience of the audience. A good shaman is an artist, perceiving the emotional state of the other, responding empathically, and communicating his response by arranging symbols, known to both, that will shift the other's perceptions and mood.

Actually this description may apply to any meaningful communication between people if the word "symbol" is defined as language, even though most everyday conversations between Sharanahua as between ourselves are merely a conventional exchange of words, serving a multitude of functions. The symbols used between the shaman and a sick person are images of animals, plants, objects, and people. They are symbols since they carry meaning, but like the symbols of dream and myth, they are saturated with overlapping significance. One cannot translate these symbols by one-to-one meaning like words in a dictionary, rather they are complexes of mood, concept, and need, condensed into a symbol such as the land turtle, the tapir, or an airplane.

These symbols appear in the songs that the shaman chants when he is curing. There are songs about every variety of plantain and manioc currently grown as well as varieties that used to be raised. There are chants about animals, fish, turtles, rainbows, clouds, people, swamps, and rivers. There are several specific songs for each and every symptom and ailment: simple diarrhea and bloody diarrhea, stomach aches, liver aches, vomiting, snakebite, fever, headache, ant bite, and old-age bone aches. Grippe is defined, probably accurately, as a Peruvian disease, and the songs to cure it are of Peruvian objects: bead necklaces, airplanes, motor boats, and radios.

Although there are innumerable songs, the underlying methods of communication vary only slightly from song to song. In part, many songs are based on fairly simple associations, such as singing of the swamp in relation to old-age bone aches. The drying up of the swamp is tied to the warming and easing of the aching bones. The song of the bead necklace connects the ease of the bead sliding down the thread with the ease of the passage of food down a sore throat.

> Spirit woman made it, with her hands she made it.
> She was sewing white thread through the eyes, many were
>   sewn with a needle.
> The necklace was strong from the beads, their white eyes
>   having been sewn.
> Your throat is aching, its strong cough.
> The necklace, white thread through their eyes, the beads
>   keep going down the thread.
> Your chest is hurting. I will sing and clean it well.
> My song has done it. I am cleaning it, all your flesh.
> My song is cooling, I have finished.

The songs of animals seem to stress a transfer of power from the shaman to the sick person. There is a build up of the animal's strength, his fire, his power. Then this power is transmitted to the listener by means of the animal's fat, which is symbolically applied to the patient, usually to cleanse him. The shaman, drunk on *shori,* fills himself with this power, which he is then able to transmit to the patient who, lying sick and frightened, is emotionally sustained by the shaman's strength.

> The tapir stands on his night path, along the night path the tapir goes.
> The tapir stands, his fat, his dark fat.
> The tapir goes along, his hooves on the ground.
> His belly is fat.
> His teeth, his white teeth.
> I am curing, the drunkenness comes.
> The tapir's fat, his strong dark fat is dripping.
> Your stomach aches, it is boiling.
> The tapir's blood was coming strong.
> The tapir's tail, his white feet.
> The tapir's fat, his strong fat, strong for cleaning your stomach ache.
> His fat like soap, strong fat soap, your stomach no longer boils.

Another theme, expressed in the structure and imagery of some songs, is sexual. The songs of plants growing, of branches rising strong, intermingling with leaves, and the dew starting to fall, unite the patient and the shaman in a shared experience, all the more intense for being slightly below the level of consciousness.

> Long ago our people were growing red* plantains in the garden.
> Shoots cut from the trunk were put in the ground.
> The shoots having grown up, branching, red plantains began to ripen, running with much juice, their colored juice.
> The sprout having grown up, the red plantain bore its fruit, growing from the trunk, hanging toward the ground.

* The word translated here as "red," also has the meaning of "blood" or "juice."

The red plantain tree has many leaves.
The large leaves, the round leaves grew dark.
The round leaves were moving, the plantain leaves, the
dew was falling upon them.

New songs are created by the shamans out of their own
observations and experiences and become part of the song inventory to be passed on to the next generation. Ndaishiwaka
was once flown to the missionaries' base near the large town of
Pucallpa. There for the first time, he saw large boats, far bigger
than anything that could navigate the Upper Purús. He created
a song, based on the pattern of the song of the tapir with
images describing the motions of fish, in which the power of the
motor and the strength of Peruvians are combined. The grease
of the motor replaced the fat of the animal.

New songs become as much a part of the traditional
knowledge as the old. Ndaishiwaka told me that he had learned
the song of the radio from Forako, when he first became a shaman,
yet the two-way radio the song describes has only appeared in
this region during the past fifteen years, too late for the time of
Ndaishiwaka's apprenticeship.

Its Peruvian made it, the radio is talking.
The Peruvian handles it, talking on the radio, its owner
made it.
The Peruvian was listening to many calls, the radio is
talking.
Its white antenna,* its fiery antenna up in the air.
Its owner is talking, its fiery antenna, its fire talks.
The fire light goes on, the listening, there listening, its
owner talking, many calls from there.
The white antenna in the air, many people it is calling.

The shaman's song and vision are based on the sick person's

* The word used for "antenna" is the word for "tendon."

symptoms and dreams. The sick man phrases his emotions in dreams, selecting from the stream of remembered dream imagery one or more symbols that he has heard in the shamans' songs through a hundred nights of curing vigils. The words of these songs are esoteric and metaphorical and supposedly understood only by the shamans, yet the meanings slide through, and the symptoms with which certain songs are associated are understood. The dreamer produces his dream images and, perhaps, even his pain in accord with the songs. His dream is a statement of his fears and anxiety.

The shaman takes from the dream the symbols that seem most meaningful and creates in the *shori* vision a fuller expression of the symbol he has selected. Thus, Ndaishiwaka sees the monkey of which Chicolopez has dreamed and adds that the monkey is attacking him. Tomuha has dreamed of sitting alone on a high bank; it is the shaman who adds that a Culina is killing her. The shaman then manipulates the vision. He threatens the monkey spirits that would eat Chicolopez, or, seeing his father gorge himself upon watermelons, spirit fruits that make him vomit, admonishes his father as he would a child to stop eating. Often, merely the power of the shaman's song makes the plane vanish, the sun spirit fall down cooling, or the bead necklace disappear.

While dream and vision symbolism among the Sharanahua does not involve a one-to-one relationship of meaning and symbol, neither is there completely free rein for idiosyncratic dreaming or hallucinating. Both shaman and patient are bound by the limits of the curing song structure of symbol and symptoms. A patient who dreamed of a bead necklace after cutting his foot would not be communicating since he would have chosen a symbol that is not appropriate for his symptoms. A shaman who selected the image of a land turtle from the dream of a patient suffering from headache and fever would not be talking the patient's language. Yet there is sufficient overlap and redundance of symbols, especially with regard to the most common, serious ailments for individual feelings to be expressed by the patient and picked up by the shaman.

Sharanahua shamans like shamans everywhere are usually successful in their cures. But, it has been shown that almost any method of curing that is not actually deterimental to health will relieve symptoms most of the time if the patient believes in it. The question to raise is not how this system works to effect a cure, but rather what kind of message is communicated between patient and shaman. The answer appears in the context in which the shaman is called.

The state summed up by the phrase, "He wants to die," appears to be a combination of fear and anxiety. A Sharanahua shows that he wants to die by refusing to eat, and his circle of kin chant, "My child is dying." Thus, Bashundi was bitten on the foot by a snake one afternoon. The women of the household surrounded her with the wailing, and, frightened, I asked someone to bring a large pot of water in which to immerse her foot. Basta agreed that the missionary had saved someone by this treatment, but no one moved so I went to fetch the water myself. We put Bashundi's foot into the cold water, and Basta gave her a spoonful of Peruvian snake bite remedy. The wailing continued for a while longer, and I gradually realized that there was no swelling around the bite and finally asked what kind of snake had bitten her. Bashundi's mother described a white snake about two feet long, and I walked over to Basta's house to ask if such a snake was poisonous. He assured me that it was not and that there was no danger. The weeping and chanting are ritualized responses to the sick person's emotional state, rather than a clinical judgment as to the odds against him.

The same chant is sung when a Sharanahua leaves his village to travel far away. The statement represents an experience of separation from the kin group, inflicted upon him or strongly desired, and the sick person's dream expresses some feeling of anxiety, of alienation from the world around him.

The shaman's choice of symbol and vision is based on his perception of how to diminish this alienation. The animal images may represent some view of the difficult nature of dealing with the people in one's social world. Images of Culina or *yura futsa* or Peruvian things may express curiosity about the outside world, leading away from the closed circle of kin. The shaman enters the dream, controls the animal spirits, and rescues his patient from the deadly interaction with strangers.

The choice of shamanism is a personal one. It is the only role at Marcos that is not set by kinship. It brings respect as well as dread from others but no practical reward unless one cures a foreigner. From what I know of Ndaishiwaka, it seems that a shaman combines an unusual curiosity for what lies beyond his horizon, for which he searches through *shori*, with a need to create. An artistic impulse to share his own perceptions and those of others, which has no outlet at Marcos besides shamanism. Ndaishiwaka is an expert at the art of intense direct communication. The case of Tomuha was described to me with particular care, and it is difficult for me to convey in words the clarity with which he described his vision and the emotional impact, emphasized dramatically by a touch, of his reassurance, "You will not die, Tomuha." I heard only the report of a vision that had occurred over a year previously. The impact would be far more intense during an actual cure, when a patient listens to the shaman describe a vision which is constructed of symbols from the patient's dream.

Ndaishiwaka decided to be a shaman when he was about eighteen years old. He had taken *shori* many times and had overcome his first terror of the frightening hallucinations of snakes before he decided to become a shaman. He had been bitten by a venomous snake and wanted to die. Two shamans, Forako, his father's brother, and Casha, cured him, and he desired to learn. He maintained a strict diet and celibacy during the period of his apprenticeship, although his wife objected strenuously. A snake's tongue was rubbed over him, and he ate the heart of a boa constrictor. Forako and Casha taught him all the curing songs, and as he took *shori,* he gradually began to see more elaborate visions. After about a year he returned to normal life and the practice of shamanism.

It is, perhaps, through the experience of his own fear of death and the enforced isolation and deprivation of his apprenticeship that the shaman learns to perceive in others what he has found within himself. He learns through the older shamans the images of the curing songs and the increased ability to call the spirits through *shori* hallucinations of these images. He would also experience the effect of the older shamans' ability to communicate to him through his own cure and training. He must learn to associate particular images with particular ailments and respond to his patient's fears by reexperiencing what he has known himself and then expressing it in visions and songs.

Only Culina sorcery, the throwing of *dori,* the magical substance that kills, is beyond the reach of the shaman. The suspicion of Culina sorcery is raised particularly when anyone becomes sick who has had any contact with them. If, as in the case of Tomuha, only a small amount of *dori* has been thrown into the person, it is still possible to cure, but more *dori* makes recovery hopeless. The person will either die, or, if taken to the Culina village in time, may be cured by Shoaki, the Culina shaman. I think that the belief in Culina sorcery is strongly promulgated by the Sharanahua shamans. Not only does it provide a useful excuse for failing to cure, but more importantly it shields the shamans from the suspicion that they have caused death by their control of spirits. Ndaishiwaka admitted to having killed two people by singing them to death, but he considered both killings justifiable since they were in revenge for murders. He advised me that, even though he had taught me the songs which can kill by causing a disease instead of curing, I would be unable to use them since women cannot be shamans and only shamans can control the spirits.

Ndaishiwaka described to me a spirit that he could call, a human spirit, who lives in the world below ours. His name is Chato, and he wears a woven shirt and penis belt and has beautiful paint. He is handsome, but his feet are hard and curled under, and he cannot move. In part, this is the transformation of an old memory, although Ndaishiwaka says he never met such a person except through *shori*. A year after this image was described, however, Yawandi, remembering scenes of her own past, surprised me by saying that when she was about five years old, she met an older brother of Zacharais and was frightened. His name was Chato; he was handsome, but he had, in her description, what must have been club feet.

For Ndaishiwaka this image is a personal one, which may find its way into myth, but probably not into the curing songs. It is a startling and lucid self-image of Ndaishiwaka—beautiful, wise, yet unable to move out of the confines of his society to a world he can see beyond him. The transformation necessary to bring Chato to his feet in the real world is the break with Sharanahua society that Ndaishiwaka longs for, is terrified of, and which, most likely, will never occur. It is the longing plus the ability of expression that mark him as a shaman, and it is this pull away from his own society and his powers within it that make the shaman feared.

In myths shamans are evil and dangerous, potential cannibals like Ruapitsi, who ate one wife and cut off pieces from his own thigh for food. His second wife killed him with an axe, and when her brothers came for her they saw with horror, "pepper, fish drugs, poison—he was a true shaman."

Basta told the story of how Yapi, the Mouse-Spirit, taught her human cousin to give birth. Mouse, who had had a great many children herself, taught the woman how to push, how the water bag would break, how the cord should be tied and the placenta delivered. Before this, children had been born by cutting women open, the way a fetal peccary is taken from its dead mother, and the shaman, hungry for blood, was angry when he found he could no longer eat the placenta, the umbilical cord, and the woman's fat.

Yawandi told me another story in which one man killed another. When I asked her why, since in most stories there is a reason given for killing, she replied that the killer was a shaman, therefore he liked to kill. When I questioned further, thinking perhaps I had misunderstood or that there were different kinds of shamans, she answered that she meant men like Ndaishiwaka or Casha or Baido. Men who take part in everyday life, yet have the power to call the spirits, and no one can be sure if they call them for good or for evil, to cure or to kill.

The shaman is at the same time an intrinsic member of Sharanahus society and a man who travels through *shori* beyond the kinship barrier. He is the jaguar, man-like, predatory, the figure with which women threaten their children—"Come here, the jaguar will take you"—and the child clings to its mother in fear. The shaman keeps the barrier of kinship intact by prowling its fences and finding the breaks through which people peer out. Terrified by the loss of security involved in feeling separated from one's kin, a Sharanahua seeks traffic with the jaguar, who represents the childhood terror, yet is also a man who knowing the lure and danger of that world beyond, takes him back to the secure confines of his kin group.

ESPERANZA

Confrontation with the Peruvian World

Long before the sound has reached my ears, the children say, "*motore*," and we begin to watch the river. Often a full fifteen minutes goes by before a shape appears around the curve of the river moving upstream toward Marcos, and it is identified as Linde, one of the traders. The children flock to Basta's port, and when Linde finally stops the motor and ties the boat to the pole, Basta and Gustavo are there to shake hands like Peruvians and greet him in Spanish, "Buenos días, Don Linde." Linde greets some men by name, others he calls *chai,* a term which several of the traders have adopted for addressing Indian men.

While Baiyakondi and Tundo hastily hide the supper we were eating as Linde walks by, Basta gives Linde a plateful of food. As men begin to drift over to where Linde and Basta are sitting, Linde offers a bottle of *cachasa,* a raw rum that sears the throat and is estimated at 140 proof. Linde has brought several bottles, and Gustavo and Zacharais agree to buy some. The bottles are passed from hand to hand as each man takes a sip. A few more bottles are sold, and the men start to call Linde, *chai,* and bring over ocelot and jaguar skins for his inspection. They laugh and joke with Linde and repeat the prices he mentions. The men know the price of first-class and second-class skins; they know the prices of peccary and deer skins, even though most of them are unable to add. When Linde suggests what goods and what debts a skin will pay for, there is no way in which they can check it.

Ndaishiwaka gets drunker and drunker, and Linde, who has been told by another man that Ndaishiwaka has a first-class ocelot skin, keeps asking to see it. Ndaishiwaka has been planning to hold this skin to trade to Renee for a new shotgun, but Linde is now his *compañero* and, despite Chatafundia's protests and pleading, he takes the rolled-up skin down from the rafter and brings it to Linde. Several more bottles of cachasa come off the price of the skin and are rapidly consumed by the men sitting at Basta's house. Their voices are far louder than usual, their movements more aggressive. Only Linde drinks moderately. Only he is clear headed next morning as he leaves Marcos, while Ndaishiwaka is sick and glum, saddened that two pairs of slacks, two shirts, and a length of cloth are all he has to show for the ocelot skin.

The dry season is the time when traders frequent Marcos, cruising up river in the *peque-peques,* to buy jaguar and ocelot skins. They bring with them a chest full of cloth, shells, and other items which may be desired by the Sharanahua. They extend credit on the promise that a skin will be forthcoming. Shamarua, Sharafo, Tohukai, Iconahua, and other men go far up the Purús, searching for jaguars. One jaguar skin will buy a shotgun or a transistor radio. Iconahua once brought in a jaguar skin with which he bought one of the two or three battery-powered phonographs in the entire region. There was unfortunately only one record available, which he played until it wore out.

Increasingly, trade goods have become necessities in the lives of the Sharanahua, whose original interest in obtaining machetes and shotguns has broadened to include such essential items as clothes and *mosquiteros,* needles and thread for sewing, metal pots, soap, matches, and men's shoes and hats. In addition, the Sharanahua buy many luxury items. These include flashlights and batteries, kerosene for small lamps, lipstick used for face painting, belts, and sunglasses.

The Sharanahua have only a few opportunities and methods for earning money to pay for any of these items. The most common source of income is skins. The skins that are saleable are those of the jaguar, ocelot, white-lipped peccary, collared peccary, and deer. Of these, the latter three are from animals whose meat is eaten regularly. These skins are worth only a little. A collared peccary skin sells for 20 *soles* (80¢) in Esperanza, a deer skin for 10 *soles* (40¢), and a white-lipped peccary skin for 5 *soles* (20¢). These prices compare poorly to those for jaguar skins, which, depending on size and quality, bring in between 1200 and 1600 *soles*.

For the younger men another occasional source of income is working on the traders' gardens in Esperanza for a week or two. Supposedly they earn 25 *soles* per day, but since the traders pay in goods rather than cash, the actual payment is rather less than this. A man will work five days for a pair of slacks and three days for a shirt. The slacks are worth 60 *soles,* the shirt 50 *soles*. However, the trader is expected to give meals since the Indian is living away from his own village. Travel time is, of course, not paid. Occasionally there is a need for workers to build or repair a house for a trader or the Dominican priest.

During the dry season, turtle eggs are taken into Esperanza for sale. Turtles are bought by passing traders who keep them alive until they wish to eat them. Marcos is too far from Esperanza for the regular sale of meat, fish, or crops, though when traders pass through the village they buy meat for their dinner. A few men, however, are beginning to sell *fariña,* roasted manioc flour, and Baiyakondi grows rice for one of the traders.

Women earn a small amount of money by selling an occasional chicken or duck for 20 *soles* and eggs at 1 *sol* apiece. These are bought by the traders for their own consumption. The quantity sold by the entire village of Marcos is approximately two chickens or one chicken and one duck a month. Approximately fifteen to twenty eggs are sold within a month to the Peruvians, the missionaries, and the anthropologist.

Sharanahua and Peruvians confront one another with several sets of misperceptions on both sides. Each sees through the lenses of his own culture and carries expectations foreign to the other. From the Sharanahua point of view Peruvians are *nawa*, inhuman but powerful. Placing Peruvians outside of predictable human nature, makes it difficult or impossible to figure out which trader is more honest or who is the worst crook. At times Sharanahua are led by their own desires to expect incredible generosity from the trader. Perhaps one trader will give away what he has instead of holding them to their debts. Traders have a quantity of goods, an ability to get a seemingly inexhaustible supply, that would lead a generous man to make gifts. The Sharanahua's own system of reciprocity involves a mutual dependence. While one does not continue to give to someone who never reciprocates, one does not carefully make an accounting of exactly what must be repaid. One may, like Basta, be proud of often giving more than others.

A Sharanahua, wishing to end a reciprocal relationship, stops giving, but Peruvians do not easily accept being stuck with a bad debt. Traders complain that they give away shells and flashlights and that Sharanahua refuse to hunt jaguars to repay them. In fact, Sharanahua find repaying distasteful and much prefer to take a jaguar skin to a trader with whom they have no debts so that they will receive more trade goods. There are no "pure" economic relationships at Marcos. Often I have found this one of the most exhausting features of life at Marcos. If, for example, I decide that I want an egg, I must consider whether it will be worth several hours of my time and a difficult and tricky interpersonal scene in which we must figure out what will be acceptable in return and how to politely defend my possessions from what seem to me inordinate demands of return. On the other hand, I do not wish to be considered stingy or insult the person by too small a return. One does not, at Marcos, walk over to someone and simply say, "I want two eggs." Instead, one waits around the house and often enough someone will figure out what you are waiting for or needing. Or else, one goes to someone's house and says, "I have come to talk with you." The visit goes on until either the subject comes up or one vaguely talks around it.

After every field trip I have spent a few days relishing the impersonality of buying and selling in Pucallpa. One may be polite and add words of greeting while purchasing, but it is not essential to the operation. Nor need one maintain any relationship after the purchase has been made.

The traders know what they are doing when they give and sell *cachasa* before buying an ocelot skin. It is not simply to confuse or muddy a Sharanahua's head with drink, but it is to set up a relationship for the moment, in which it appears that the trader is giving and good, and the Sharanahua will feel that this time this unpredictable trader will give him everything he wants in exchange for a skin. The traders do not consider this dishonest, they are planning after all to pay for the skin or put credit toward an old debt.

The Sharanahua, however, who begins to believe that more than a straight (however crooked) economic transaction is going on is for a while misled into believing that social bonds now tie him to the trader. In the past, the disillusionment following such a belief led to murdering the trader. Nowadays, when the Sharanahua fear retaliation and have learned that one does not kill a Peruvian with impunity, it leads to concealed anger, frustrated rage that comes out in the avoidance of debt by cheating the trader, the angry threats uttered during drinking bouts, and the visions of spirits of Peruvians in the trance of *shori*.

A few years ago, Ndaishiwaka was angered by a trader's low price for a jaguar skin. Thinking of the skill and the danger of taking a jaguar, faced with what he felt was a poor exchange,

Ndaishiwaka skinning an ocelot

he cut the skin up and fashioned a belt while the trader stood by and cursed him. For the Sharanahua the jaguar is a symbol of many ideas, only one of which is the possibility of gain. In myths the jaguar is the dangerous stranger, the devourer. Within memory, before shotguns became common, jaguars used to stalk the nearby gardens and approached the villages at night, and women hushed a crying child, whispering, "Be quiet, the jaguar will take you!" And still today as one walks a forest trail and hears a sound far off, Sharanahua freeze in place and whisper, "*Basharo!*" "Jaguar!"

Years ago jaguars were stabbed to death with the decorated spears of hard palm wood that the Sharanahua used for war. Ordinary game was taken with bows and arrows, but men and jaguars were killed with spears. Jaguars, like men, are predators, the only important predators of the tropical forest. In a real sense jaguars are competitors for meat, stalking game by night as men stalk by day. In another sense, because he is a competitor, the jaguar, like all strangers, is dangerous and should be killed before he attacks.

Sharanahua men have always hunted jaguars and ocelots, priding themselves in the past on hats and belts made of their pelts. Today the Sharanahua wear Peruvian-style clothing and trade jaguar skins for credit with which to purchase trade goods. Nowadays jaguars and ocelots are taken in baited traps, fashioned like boxes with one end tied up to leave an entrance. As the jaguar enters, hungrily seizing the bait, he triggers the cord, and the box closes. The hunter then strangles the jaguar with a noose or carefully places a shot through its eye so that the skin will not lose its price by showing pellet holes.

Jaguar and ocelot skins are the only items the Sharanahua can obtain that are highly valued by traders. For the backwoods traders of the Upper Purús, jaguars represent a road to riches which will somehow, someday, make them rich enough to buy a house in Lima. It has never happened, but the dream of quick wealth is the illusion that holds them in the backwaters of Peru. Thus, Don Ciro, one of the traders in Esperanza, remembers as the high point of his life the time he had a job going from Iquitos to Miami shipping tropical fish. He dreams of collecting all his debts, a mythical sum of 70,000 *soles* owed to him by numerous Indians, and returning to live in Pucallpa or Iquitos. He cannot afford the trip to Pucallpa more than a couple of times a year so he must sell the skins to Gamboa, the biggest trader of the Upper Purús. In order to make any profit, Ciro must go upriver to buy skins where he will pay less. He pays in goods, which he in turn has bought from Gamboa. In the three years I have spent near Esperanza, Ciro has almost died twice. Once he turned over in his canoe while paddling alone at night during the height of the rainy season when the Purús turns mud color and speeds huge logs along its current. He prayed to his saint to save him, promising to repay the saint with a party if he lived. The second time was the summer of 1969 when he cut his leg open while buying skins up on the Embira. His leg swelled and for six days his life depended on Tararai, a Sharanahua, who had been hired to accompany him.

Señor Gamboa is a man from the sierra. Rumor has it that he is an exconvict. He mixes unctiousness with contempt when speaking to anyone he considers of a higher social class than himself, but to all others only contempt and a conviction of his own power is communicated. Gamboa is rich by the standards of Esperanza. He is the only trader who can afford to charter a plane to transport his cargo of goods into Esperanza and to ship his skins back to Pucallpa.

Gamboa makes it clear to the other traders that he is the strong man of Esperanza. His dream is of power, and he seeks to eliminate the other traders from Esperanza so that he alone can control trade and prices, so that Indians such as the Sharanahua will be unable to take their trade elsewhere. Throughout the Peruvian *selva* there are such men, the strong *patróns* who control Indians through debt peonage. Only Don Enrique Echigeray still questions Gamboa's place in the pecking order, but Echigeray is another dreamer who still cherishes his motorcycling trophy and has put all his money into a huge launch that he has planned to take up to Iquitos. He would sell it and make his fortune, leaving Esperanza far behind. The launch has sat unmoving for over a year. Echigeray sneers at Gamboa, but not when he faces him since often he must swallow his pride and buy from Gamboa himself. One night Echigeray and Gamboa got drunk together and began to brag about how much money each had. Echigeray leaped to his feet, ran back to his house, and brought all his money with him. He counted it out and waited for Gamboa to do the same. Gamboa won.

There are other traders in Esperanza: Renee who is soft spoken and his sons, one of whom speaks the language of the Indians and knows their culture well. Renee's son took Alberto, a Sharanahua, to hunt jaguars on the Embira and when Alberto died there after three days of a severe case of dysentery,

Tararai

he easily convinced Alberto's people that the Culina had done the killing by throwing *dori*. The Culina, who were also working for the trader, denied this killing and feared that the Sharanahua would revenge his death.

When Ciro, the trader, was ill, Tararai carried him and cared for him for six days. When Alberto was sick, the trader let him die untreated and blamed it on Culina magic. Tararai worked with Ciro for two months. Ciro paid him in goods for fifteen days, claiming that he had to buy food for Tararai. Ciro paid 70 *soles* for the period that Tararai cared for him, but paid it to a distant relative who happened to be in Esperanza but never gave the money to Tararai. Ciro paid Tararai 700 *soles* for a skin that cost 900 in Esperanza. He paid, of course, in goods and claimed that the price was fair since he had bought it on the Embira not in Esperanza and would receive only the 900 *soles* from Gamboa.

Tararai thought the price was too low and traveled with me into Esperanza. He showed Echigeray how much he had been paid. Echigeray would like to take business from Ciro and Gamboa so he laughed at Tararai and told him he had been badly cheated. I went with Tararai to the *guardia civil*, the Peruvian policeman, who agreed that the skin was worth more but said it was his day off and suggested we speak to the *comandante del puesto*, the army officer in charge of the tiny frontier post. Because I was present the *comandante* agreed to listen. He called Ciro in and told him that this *cholo* and I were objecting to the price. When Ciro indignantly defended himself, the *comandante* sent for an impartial expert on the price of skins— Gamboa. Not surprisingly Gamboa supported his underling and godson, Ciro. The *comandante* with icy politeness asked if I were satisfied. I suggested that he had better ask Tararai. Only a naive anthropologist, as I was then, and an outsider to Peruvian society, like Tararai, would have expected, even for a moment, a different conclusion.

For the moment ignoring the more vicious individual traits of some traders, they are members of a society which is structured through the impersonal workings of market exchange. They buy in Pucallpa and try to pick items for which the price is low. The price of fine skins fluctuates on the international market within days or weeks. The successful traders hold their skins whenever possible for the price to go up, while making buying trips and quoting the low price to the Indians. Profit is expected on both the skins and the goods given in payment. The traders feel they are sacrificing their lives in a miserable uncivilized place, and their only self-justification is that some day they will leave as rich men.

The Sharanahua want manufactured things and are beginning to regard them as necessities. The Peruvians control these things, and their manufacture is a mystery to the Sharanahua. It is equally a mystery to most Peruvians, but they strive for money and ask no questions. The traders believe, as perhaps we do as well, that money is somehow a real thing. The Sharanahua are probably more perceptive in regarding money as a strange and power-ridden concept. They see it as a fresh idea, while we are believers, accepting without question such mystic notions as there not being enough money to build a school or a house, when in reality there are people willing to build and food to feed them. Belief systems have their own level of reality, so that if money is thought to be scarce, people are not paid, food is not bought, and schools are not built. The Shara-nahua are beginning to accept and make use of this concept, learning that money is scarce and that goods bought with money are also scarce and that, therefore, one does not share them.

It is not the things in themselves that confuse interactions and may create change at Marcos. New tools and goods may slowly shift the organization of any society, but as long as the new organization structures the same roles, the same expectations and obligations, no drastic shift in daily interactions is experienced. That is, whether women add to the definition of their role additional tasks, such as manufacturing *fariña*, or substitute this work for that of weaving cotton, whether fishing becomes more important with the use of harpoons and *tarafas* than hunting, the relationship of men to men and men to women and women to women might easily remain the same. But Peruvian things are embedded in Peruvian society and obtaining objects involves Peruvian relationships as well as Peruvian beliefs.

Tararai was not only angry about the price of the skin, but also at Ciro's contemptuous treatment of a man who had saved his life. Money is the symbol and rationalization of the structure which places Indians and poor Peruvians below the level of humans and supports the claim of the traders with the force of the *comandante*. Certainly Tararai wanted the money and the things he could buy with it, but his anger was based on experiencing the inequality of roles that characterizes Peruvian society.

A few women at Marcos have sexual relations with a

trader in exchange for trade goods such as cloth, hair dressing, or kerosene. Bashkondi and Koyo laughed at me once when I told them my kerosene stove was worthless because kerosene cost too much. "You don't understand anything," said Bashkondi. "Sleep with a *nawa* once and you'll get a liter of kerosene." Naikashu told Tarani to show me the cloth and hair dressing she was given for only a single night with Linde. Bashkondi, however, has also burst into tears of rage at Echigeray's teasing, saying, "That *nawa* has made fun of me."

Bashkondi and Koyo understand the Sharanahua battle of the sexes, but not the Peruvian. The Sharanahua battle is between equals, with little compassion, perhaps, but no contempt, and sexual relations are not viewed as a loss to the women's side. The Peruvian making a sexual conquest reduces the woman to the commodity he has given in exchange. He is the winner and she, the trophy. Sharanahua men compete with one another to gain women; Peruvian men seek a trophy to prove their superiority to other men.

In other parts of the world inequality is often ameliorated by regulation and watered down by the more humane elements of the culture. In the *selva* there is no regulation and no amelioration. Peruvian culture runs thin, attenuated in an environment that cannot support it, providing wants and needs for which there is no satisfaction, maintaining a social structure that provides a parody of class-stratified society. Esperanza could be a bearable heaven, but for many it is an isolated hell. Its name symbolizes the contradiction, meaning either "hope" or "waiting for."

Ciro brought a young wife from Pucallpa to Esperanza. She had been there about six months when I met her and stayed one night in their house. I asked her who lived in the house next to theirs on the right, some twenty feet away, and she was not sure. I asked her whose house was on the other side, and she replied that Ciro knew them, but she had never spoken to them.

Echigeray's twelve-year-old son, Enrique, returned from the Dominicans' school for lunch and kept trying to capture his father's attention to tell him about his morning at school. Echigeray said he was busy and went back to his own conversation despite his son's continuing chatter. Only when Enrique mentioned that he had known an answer that Gamboa's son had not and called the other boy "stupid" did Echigeray pay any attention. He told Enrique not to call his friend "stupid," and asked Enrique to describe the entire scene. Enrique will undoubtedly learn what his father is teaching—to compete and to win are the only important parts of experience, the reprimand for calling his friend stupid is not to be taken seriously. His father's disinterest in Enrique's learning the substance of schoolwork and his father's rapt attention to his outdoing his peer are the crucial messages.

Despite the flock of children in Esperanza, all within a minute's walk, Enrique spends time away from his house only during school hours or to play soccer in front of the school. He may walk to Gamboa's house to buy an ice and talk to Gamboa's son, but he speaks contemptuously to the shabby children of the poor Peruvians or Indians, who come to the store section of his house to buy coffee or sugar for their mothers.

Once when I flew into Esperanza and stopped by Echigeray's house to speak to his wife, she looked extremely angry and upset. She told me she had expected her husband to return from his business in Pucallpa on that plane, and he had sent no message nor money. She had run out of money and could buy no food, including the canned milk which was her nine month old's only food. There was no one she could turn to, she said, since she had no relatives in Esperanza, so I lent her the money.

Her only companions are her children and the girl who works for her, cooking and washing clothes. The servant girl or her children are sent out on errands, while she stays behind the counter of the store or in the small living quarters behind it.

If someone has brought game back to Esperanza, a child

will drop by the house to inform the Señora, and she will send the girl to purchase three kilos. However, she is unable to eat peccary, tapir, or capybara since these foods, she says, make one ill.

Esperanza, with its class structure, is a trap for the anthropologist, one that I avoided for the first two fieldtrips only to be confronted head on with assumptions I had never questioned. It was easy though infuriating to recognize my naiveté in expecting justice between a trader and an Indian. It was shattering to discover the unwitting acceptance of inequality within myself.

I have often had to spend a night or two in Esperanza, waiting for the sky to clear so a plane might land or waiting for someone to head upriver so that I could get to Marcos. I generally stayed with Echigeray and his wife, who were generous in their hospitality, providing room for my hammock and meals at their table. Aside from these stays, I avoided Esperanza as much as possible, going in only to buy coffee, sugar, sardines, and gifts once in two months.

The river trips with people from Marcos were tiring but exciting breaks in routine. We always managed to sleep at an Indian village or along the beach, spending only a few hours in Esperanza. All of us agreed that we preferred not to sleep with Peruvians in Esperanza. Yawandi traveled in with me once to have a tooth pulled by the *sanitario,* a man whose only dental skill was extraction. Ndaishiwaka and Zacharais were paddling the canoe, and we agreed as usual that we would leave Marcos at dawn, reach Esperanza in the afternoon, buy machetes for the men, buy my supplies, get Yawandi's tooth pulled, and leave to eat and sleep on a beach or travel back upriver as far as Piquinique.

As usual we left Marcos later than our plan and reached Esperanza late in the day. I rushed to buy supplies, expecting that Yawandi would finish with her tooth and we could rapidly depart. Yawandi, however, followed me to the trader's and said she could not find the *santiario*. Impatiently I searched Esperanza and within a half-hour had discovered the *sanitario*, who said it was too late to pull a tooth, that the night air would be dangerous. I dismissed that logic and tried to intimidate him, until he pointed out that it was growing dark and the kerosene lamp would not give sufficient light. I could not argue, it was obviously true, and I coldly thought that we could forget about Yawandi's tooth and leave anyway.

A moment later I became aware of my callousness. I knew that Yawandi would still be in pain, that it had taken trust for her to travel with me as her main companion, and that she had never failed me when I felt strange and bewildered at Marcos as she did now in Esperanza. I realized grudgingly that we must stay in Esperanza for the night, and we all headed toward the port, a long walk, to get our hammocks and *mosquiteros*. We walked a ways and Ndaishiwaka, who was ahead of me on the path, turned and asked, "Fando, where will you sleep?" I answered, "At Echigeray's." Ndaishiwaka stopped for a moment and turned to look at me. I felt humiliated, caught out at his recognition that I was planning to stay with a middle-class Peruvian who would never allow Indians to sleep in his home. It was a confrontation I had always avoided—to be a Sharanahua at Marcos and a middle-class foreigner at Esperanza, and I was appalled at my readiness to exchange friends whose company I enjoyed for the tedious proprieties of middle-class status. And I knew why I had always hated Esperanza.

I blurted out to Ndaishiwaka, "Where are you staying?" He answered, "At Monoco's." I asked if there would be room for me, knowing that where one can sling three hammocks there is always room for four. We took our things out of the canoe and walked back up toward Esperanza. I felt burdened, thinking of my hypocrisy, but Yawandi only asked what I would say to Echigeray. I replied that I would ask him if he wanted to take all of us into his house and that when he refused we would go to Monoco's. Then I felt light and happy, as though I had been rescued from standing close to the edge of a cliff.

Monoco and his wife let the four of us heat our food on their fire, offered us plates, gave us turtle eggs, let us eat on their floor and sling our hammocks in the room where their sons played the transistor radio all night. I woke at dawn, and Yawandi had already returned from bathing at the port. As we went to the *sanitario* the early morning sun lit the blue and green paint of the Dominicans' school and the crazy pink of the new bandstand that sits half covered with weeds in the grassy, snake-filled plaza of Esperanza, and it looked like a fairy tale.

The tiny middle class of Esperanza, the traders, the army and radio men, associate as little with the poor *selváticos* such as Monoco as they do with Indians. They are quicker to order an Indian to pick up a heavy package without pay, but they treat the poor Peruvians in a domineering fashion as well. A few of the poor Peruvians trade with the Indians, working for one of the richer traders who can afford to ship the skins out on Cívico, but most of them clear gardens, hunt, and fish, eeking out a little money by selling meat, turtle eggs, and skins. This money barely covers the cost of clothes, sugar, coffee, and other necessities, and they have little more than the Sharanahua and a poorer diet.

Monoco and his wife have had twelve children, one of whom died in an accident. No woman at Marcos works as hard as his wife, although, unlike a Sharanahua woman, agriculture, fishing, and gathering are not part of her tasks. Yet simply cooking, washing clothes, and caring for eleven children without the help of other women is an incredibly difficult job, even with the necessary assistance of her older children.

The skills of Sharanahua men are lower-class skills in Peruvian society. Getting food directly by hunting, fishing, or agriculture are skills held in low esteem, whereas selling, producing, owning, and the manipulation of money are respected. The

Sharanahua are aware of and resent the contempt that most Peruvians show to Indians. Most Sharanahua accept the Peruvian's command to pick up that carton and carry it over there. When Zacharais went to the radio shack with me, the young Peruvian ordered him to pump the generator. After a few minutes Zacharais began to tire at the hard, unfamiliar job, but obeyed the order to keep going. Young men more openly resent this type of treatment. Most Sharanahua either avoid all contacts with Peruvians or superficially accept the inferior position in which they are placed.

One of the reasons for the occasional success of missionaries is that they appear to offer a way out of this bind. They represent a sophisticated culture whose objects are desired as are the widespread world they represent and a mode of entering that world which appears to sidestep acceptance of the inferior role. Gustavo, who seeks to be a bilingual teacher and religious leader, usually avoids contact with Peruvians in Esperanza so as not to bring into question the superiority he seeks as a knower of the right path, his ability to read the Bible and be more pious than the Peruvians he seeks to emulate. Gustavo rightfully prides himself on his studies at the mission base, the hard work of learning to read his own language and Spanish. He is also proud of the transistor radio he was able to buy at the mission base and his watch and sunglasses that Peruvians wear. He is looking for a way of escaping the limits of his own culture and entering the national culture without being forced to accept the lower-class role into which Peruvians place all Indians.

While the skills of reading, writing, and basic arithmetic are indeed useful, a missionized Indian is in a precarious position. He can maintain his self-respect only by staying outside of the national society. Once the missionaries leave, taking with them the planes, the two-way radio, the medical supplies—all the factors that a man such as Gustavo views as a connection with the larger world outside—his fragile position crumbles. I

Chatafundia decorating a bow for trade with the author

have met men in other villages who have started like Gustavo but have lost their position as the mission was taken out, and they appear to have nowhere to go. The illusion they had of membership in the greater society cannot stand up to the inferior position they must accept if they take part in the national culture.

Both the success and the problem of the anthropologist are due to offering another road to the world outside. The anthropologist plays a role of equality inside the village and is at home in the world outside as well. It is less dangerous than the missionary's road only because the anthropologist stays a brief time and is seldom as well equipped with available plane service, schools, and mission bases.

The Sharanahua are attracted not only by the useful tools and glittering objects of the outside world, but by the swagger of the Peruvian, apparently in control of a larger and more exciting world, apparently moving with ease among strangers and foreigners, untrammeled by a multitude of obligations, unafraid of spirits. The Sharanahua are curious about the world outside, but it frightens them with their own beliefs about the dangers of other people not one's kin, and it presents them with an inferior role in a structure not their own.

The familiar categories still order the Sharanahua's social world, but Peruvians, today's *nawa,* will never become *yura futsa.* Occasionally a trader takes an Indian wife, but he maintains no relationship with her people. Peruvian women do not marry Indians nor can a Sharanahua imagine taking a Peruvian woman as a wife. The contact with Peruvian society, therefore, fixes these categories, gluing them to a different orientation in which Peruvians are always *nawa,* all other Indians, *yura futsa,* one's kin and one's affinals (relatives through marriage), *noko kaifo,* our people. The fluid structure is becoming solidified, and the Sharanahua must either turn away from further contact, remain rigidly unchanged and unchanging in a fixed pattern of relationships, or permit their structuring of the human world to crumble. Marcos is a moment in time, a place where one current of indigenous culture has met the resistant surface of Peruvian society.

At this point in time the Sharanahua could still withdraw from any contact with missionaries or Peruvians. They like trade goods and regard them as essential, but they have not lost the techniques that make subsistence possible without them. Older men still know how to make knives from a peccary's tooth, manufacture a fire drill, a torch of raw rubber, elaborate baskets, spears, and bows and arrows. Older women still make clay pots, and all women know how to spin and weave cotton hammocks, skirts and baby slings, baskets for carrying and serving food. The structures of village life are still viable. Yet I doubt that the Sharanahua will take this path of withdrawal. They are drawn, almost despite themselves to Peruvian life.

The Sharanahua look with longing at the larger world to meet their desires and escape their own limitations, even though the world they encounter is not their dream nor their choice. They are only partially aware of the price they will pay if they move as some men have out of the Purús to Pucallpa or Brazil to begin the transition from Indian to national. On the whole, lower-class Peruvians eat far less dependably than the Sharanahua, their children are more often sickly, they work more hours at more routinized work. They strive for higher status and more often than not are frustrated in their efforts.

I am sure, however, that even if I could convince the Sharanahua of the poor exchange they or their children or their grandchildren will make, it would not dissuade them. As an ethnographer I may be sad to see another culture vanish, another variety ground into the homogeneity of Western culture, but as a fellow human I admire that reaching out—to enter the world beyond the boundary of the *maloca*. The tragedy of Indian cultures is not their vanishing, it is the misery of the societies they enter, a tragedy in which we are also trapped. The romance of anthoropology is to find somewhere else a culture less trammeled than our own. The reality of anthropology is to take part in learning to break its confines.

The night before I left Marcos for the last time, I was awakened by a frightening din of people wailing and dogs barking. It sounded like angry spirits, and I called out to Ahui-yumba to ask what was happening. She answered, "Tsatsa's baby is dead," and for a moment I felt sick with guilt that I had never known the baby was ill. As I woke more fully, I remembered that Ahuiyumba often lied and that she had no way of being any surer than I was of what was happening. I got dressed and started to leave the house and met Samuel, returning, who told me that Baiyakondi was dying. He had been sick for days with vague stomach pains.

As I walked along the dark path, going over to Baiyakondi's house, I met Yawandi and Naikashu returning, crying. Inside Baiyakondi's *mosquitero* Shumundo and Yawanini wailed, "My child is dying, my child is dying," and Tundo sat weeping. Ndaishiwaka, stripped to the waist in the hot *mosquitero*, sang and blew smoke over Baiyakondi. Basta took my hand and pushed it deep into Baiyakondi's gut, where I could feel a pulse throbbing. I sat with Tundo until Ruapa came in to replace Ndaishiwaka, and then went outside where five men sat taking *shori*. The men chanted tensely to call the spirits that threatened Baiyakondi.

Ndaishiwaka took a bowlful of *shori* and sat quietly waiting for the vision to appear. He told me his father, Baiyakondi, had dreamed of a river, and he asked me to give his father an injection. I said that I would in the morning when there was light, though I had no reason to believe it would help. I left Marcos the next morning, after giving the injection, and will probably never know if Baiyakondi lived. No one has died during the three years I knew Marcos, yet each time the wailing begins, one fears, and death felt very close that night. I asked Ndaishiwaka what he could see, and he answered that he was seeing a river. Though I have heard the wailing for Baiyakondi many times, he is an old man and one day he will die, and his spirit, lonely and angry, will look for his kin to take with him and then fly back to his land, the Tarauacá, the river of his birth.

APPENDIX A

Glossary of animal and fish names mentioned in the text.

Agouti (Dasyprocta) A rodent weighing approximately nine pounds, resembles a large mouse or delicate rat, inhabits woods, edible.

Boca chica (Prochilodus nigricens) A fish resembling a bass, seasonally abundant in rivers and lakes, which weighs about two to three pounds. Its flesh is delicious but is filled with small bones.

Capybara (Hydrochoerus hydrochaeris) The largest living rodent, weighs between 110 and 165 pounds, aquatic, usually gregarious. Its meat is valued.

Paca (Cuniculus paca) A large rodent, about 22 pounds, inhabits woods, usually solitary, brownish fur with white markings, good eating.

Peccary (Tayassu tajacu) Collared peccary, small, about 30 to 45 pounds, solitary or travels in small bands of six to eight.
(Tayassu pecari) White-lipped peccary, 50 to 75 pounds, commonly travels in large herds. Both peccaries bear a resemblance to one's idea of a wild pig but are not closely related to domestic pigs. The meat has a very strong flavor with a faint resemblance to pork.

Paiche (Arapaima gigas) The largest fresh-water fish, referred to in the literature as *pirarucú*. It reaches 10 feet and 225 pounds. Its flesh is white, sweet, and delicious.

Tapir (Tapirus terrestris) The largest animal of the tropical forest, distantly related to the horse. It weighs about 450 to 550 pounds, inhabits woods.

APPENDIX B

Glossary of Spanish words.

Barbasco A plant cultivated to drug fish, botanically belongs to the genus Tephrosia.

Caboclo A term used generally to derogate a person of lower social class from the backwoods. The closest English equivalent would be "hick," with a racial overtone of insult.

Cholo An insulting term for an Indian attempting to pretend to higher social status or cultural knowledge as a Peruvian. (When used to a friend, it is a nickname, but it was not so used in the scene described.)

Compañero A friendly acquaintance.

Fariña A flour made from processed manioc. While generally in the literature it refers to the fine flour made from bitter varieties of manioc, in the Peruvian *selva*, it is an extremely crude (about the consistency of grapenuts) substance made from sweet manioc (*yuca*).

Huaca A plant cultivated to drug fish, botanically belongs to the genus Tephrosia.

Maloca A word, derived originally from a widespread Indian language, that has entered Spanish and anthropological vocabularies. It most frequently refers to a large, communal house.

Mosquitero A heavy cotton mosquito net, large enough to stand in, which not only protects from insects but provides warmth and privacy.

Sanitario A para-medical, paid by the government to give treatment in poor and rural areas.

Selva The word means "forest." In Peru it is applied to the entire area of the tropical forest. One is inevitably told that there are three regions in Peru: *la costa*, "the coast," *la sierra*, "the highlands," *la selva*, "the forest."

Selvático. A native of the *selva*. This does not refer specifically to Indians, but generally to those born in the tropical forest zone.

Tambo A temporary shelter.

Tarafa A Peruvian fish net made of strong string with heavy weights. It is dropped open from a boat and pulled closed when a fish is taken.

APPENDIX C

The title of the book is taken from the following passage in *The German Ideology*:

> For as soon as the distribution of labour comes into being, each man has a particular, exclusive sphere of activity, which is forced upon him and from which he cannot escape. He is a hunter, a fisherman, a shepherd, or a critical critic, and must remain so if he does not want to lose his means of livelihood; while in communist society, where nobody has one exclusive sphere of activity but each can become accomplished in any branch he wishes, society regulates the general production and thus makes it possible for me to do one thing today and another tomorrow, to hunt in the morning, fish in the afternoon, rear cattle in the evening, criticise after dinner, just as I have a mind, without ever becoming hunter, fisherman, shepherd or critic.*

The notes that follow give sources, additional data, and clarification of some interpretations that would be of interest to students of anthropology and anthropologists, but are not essential to an understanding of the text. These notes are organized in terms of topics that appear in each chapter, but they are not footnoted in the text itself.

* Karl Marx and Frederick Engels, *The German Ideology*, C. J. Arthur, ed., New York: International Publishers, 1970, p. 53.

Chapter One

1. Many Sharanahua have taken Spanish names, although only a few men use them. All of the Sharanahua have several Indian names. Throughout the book I have used whichever name was most frequently applied to each individual. A few names have been changed in the text, where the information given seems potentially embarrassing or damaging.

2. The Sharanahua refer to their own language as "speech" or "language." The Summer Institute of Linguistics calls this language "Marinahua," and it is discussed in the following publications: Scott, Eugene, and Pike, Eunice, "The phonological hierarchy of Marinahua," *Phonetica* 8:1-8, 1962; Shell, Olive, "Grupos idiomáticos de la selva peruana," Lima: Publicaciones del Instituto de Filología de la Facultad de Letras de la Universidad Mayor de San Marcos, *Estudios,* No. 7, 1959; Shell, Olive, *Pano Reconstruction,* doctoral dissertation, University of Pennsylvania, 1965.

My spelling of Sharanahua is inconsistent. A few names are spelled as I first took them down in the field, before I had the opportunity to study the analysis of Marinahua phonemics and before my ear was sharp enough to catch the phonetics. Most spellings have been improved, but a few familiar names remain. In part I have followed the spelling used by the Summer Institute of Linguistics, in part I have retained a certain amount of phonetic spellings, especially for names. A reader interested in this language may consult the sources listed above. A guide to a few features of pronunciation and notation follows.

mb and *nd* are each single phonemes: Before an oral vowel they are pronounced *b* and *d* as in Bashkondi and Ndaishiwaka; they are pronounced *mb* or *nd* when in the middle of a word, such as Yawa*nd*i or bi*mb*iki; they are pronounced as *m* or *n* when they occur before nasalized vowels, as in shi*m*a (fish) or ma*n*ia (banana or plantain).

u is used for the phonetic symbol *i̵*.

f is a bilabial voiceless fricative; before *a* and *u* it is labialized, resembling the sound *hw*.

sh except before *i* is usually the retroflex *ṣh*.

r is a voiced flap.

Other consonants are roughly equivalent to English; vowels approximate standard Spanish, but neither nasalization nor tone is indicated.

3. The age at menarche is assumed to be 15 or 16, following the estimates made in a study of the Cashinahua, a closely related group living within this region, by Johnston, F. E. *et al.* "The population structure of the Peruvian Cashinahua: demographic, genetic, and cultural, interrelationships," *Human Biology* 41:29-41, 1969.

Chapter Two

1. Population figures, Marcos 1966

	Males	Females
46–65	4	1
36–45	3	5
26–35	4	9
16–25	9	9
6–15	11	11
0–5	17	6

Ages have been approximated by assuming that a woman gives birth to her first child at 18. This is based on the onset of menarche at 16 (see Note 3 for Chapter One) and a two-year period of either adolescent sterility (see Montagu, Ashley, *Adolescent Sterility*, Springfield: Charles C. Thomas, Publisher, 1946) or the practice of abortion. If conception does occur before a girl is considered to have reached her full growth, abortion will be carried out since the Sharanahua believe that pregnancy will endanger the development of the girl. There is generally a two-year period of continuing growth in adolescence after the onset of puberty, so that 18 seems a reasonable age for a first pregnancy. (Abortion is discussed in the notes for Chapter Eight.)

Despite the remarkable proportion of boys to girls in the 0–5 age group, I have no indication of or evidence for female infanticide, or any infanticide except possibly one case that was reported to me as a miscarrage in which the embryo had a foot deformity. I was not in the field at this time. Since I was freely informed about abortion, I do not think this is a case of concealing information.

Also, a tendency toward female infanticide should effect the age groups above this youngest group as well, and they are perfectly even. However, a somewhat similar sex ratio in the early years was reported for the Cashinahua for whom infanticide is reported. See Johnston *et al.*, "The population structure of the Peruvian Cashinahua."

Aside from the small numbers involved, which make it difficult to derive population dynamics, the epidemics occuring fifteen to twenty years ago have further effected the population picture.

2. For an historical and comparative analysis of the Panoan language family, see Shell, *Pano Reconstruction.*

3. For a discussion of the culture history and ecology of the Amazon Basin, see Carneiro, Robert, "The transition from hunting to horticulture in the Amazon Basin," *International Congress of Anthropological and Ethnological Sciences* (8th, Tokyo, 1968), Science Council of Japan, 1970, pp. 244–48; Lathrap, Donald, *The Upper Amazon,* London: Thames & Hudson, 1970. An article that has been crucial for studying tropical forest cultural adaptation is Carneiro, Robert, "Slash-and-burn agriculture: a closer look at its implications for settlement patterns," in Wallace, Anthony, ed., *Men and Cultures; Selected Papers of the International Congress of Anthropological and Ethnological Sciences* (5th, Philadelphia, 1956), Philadelphia: University of Pennsylvania, 1960, pp. 229–34.

Useful sources for the ecology of tropical forest flora and fauna are, Federov, An. A., "The structure of the tropical rain forest and speciation in the humid tropics," *Journal of Ecology* 54:1–11, 1966; Fittkau, Ernst *et al.*, *Biogeography and Ecology in South America,* The Hague: Junk, 1969.

4. While peanuts are a high protein crop and maize provides some proteins, the usual vegetable diet of tropical forest people is considered insufficient without the addition of animal proteins (including fish), especially where manioc is the staple of the diet. For students of tropical forest agriculture, two sources are particularly useful: Rogers, David, "Some botanical and ethnological considerations of *Manihot esculenta*," *Economic Botany* 19:369–77, 1965; Jones, William, *Manioc in Africa,* California: Stanford University

Press, 1959. In addition, the works of Carneiro and Lathrap cited above discuss the necessity for protein sources.

5. The statement of similarity between arrow types within a cultural region of linguistic diversity is taken from Lyon, Patricia, "A comparative study of the arrows of the Peruvian Montaña," unpublished manuscript.

6. Chandless, W., "Ascent of the River Purús," *Journal of the Royal Geographic Society* 35:86–118, 1866, describes the *malocas* along this part of the river. The publications of Tastevin and Rivet that deal with the region where the Sharanahua place themselves in the early 1900s are: Rivet, Paul and P. C. Tastevin, "Les tribus indiennes du Purús, de Juruá et des régions limitrophes," *La Géographie* 35:449–82, 1921; Tastevin, P. C., "Quelques considérations sur les Indiens du Juruá," *Bulletin de la Société d'Anthropologie*, ser. 6, 10:144–54, 1919; Tastevin, P. C., "Les études ethnographiques et linguistiques du P. Tastevin en Amazonie," *Journal de la Société des Américanistes*, N. S. 16:421–5, 1924; Tastevin, P. C., "Le haut Taruacá," *La Géographie* 45:34–54, 158–75, 1926.

7. A population expert, J. V. Neel, based his estimate of population trends for another South American group on the ratio of adults to children. Thus, finding 108 adults to 70 children, he suggests that "the population appears to be at least replacing itself" (p. 127). Neel, J. V. *et al.*, "Studies on the Xavante Indians of the Brazilian Mato Grosso," *American Journal of Human Genetics* 16:52–140, 1964. At Marcos the number of adults (those over the age of 15) as compared to the number of children in 1966 was 44 adults to 45 children, a figure that seems to indicate, therefore, a tendency toward population growth. In addition, by 1968 nine more live births had occurred and no deaths, with the exception of one still-born infant.

Chapter Three

1. In discussing kinship I decided not to use the terms "cross" and "parallel" for cousins since this easily misleads the nonanthropological reader into believing that the people themselves make this

distinction. Since parallel cousins are referred to and addressed by sibling terms, the word "cousin" always refers to a cross-cousin.

2.   Kinship terms: (following pages).

3.   The analysis of kinship terms is a conservative and traditional one, which has begun to trouble me. Although the Sharanahua system analyzes easily as a perfect moiety and brother-sister exchange structure, the assumption of patrilineal descent groups is a true but insufficient explanation of the total structures underlying observable behavior. There is definitely a patrilineal tinge to the naming of children and in being defined as a Sharanahua. In terms of behavior, however, it seems very doubtful that women regard their children as members of another descent group or that children regard their mothers as affines (as in the very useful approach of Dumont, Louis, "The Dravidian kinship terminology as an expression of marriage," *Man* 54:34–9, 1953). For example, Shomoni's "error" (p. 64), when he called a "mother" a "sister," indicates that the descent criteron was extremely weak, otherwise the transformation of generation would have put "mother" into a cross-cousin category.

It is possible to analyze the kinship system as one in which there is complete discord between men and women (trouble descent rather than double descent), so that women consider their children to be in *their* descent group, that is, the one of their own mothers, sisters, and mother's brothers, while men regard their children as members of *their* descent group, including fathers, brothers, and father's sisters. In the vocative terms this would be consistent with women calling their children *uwa* and *koka,* men calling their children *upa* and *achi.* A child presumably would regard himself as a member of a group consisting of parents, parents' siblings, as well as his/her own siblings.

Future research is needed to investigate this possibility. It would, if supported, provide an excellent reason for the ubiquity of bifurcate-merging systems since a world view different for each sex seems far more usual in primitive societies than a moiety system. Further, initiation ceremonies would make sense, if their distribution worked out, as a means of establishing clear-cut descent groupings and social agreement about them in a situation where none exists.

KINSHIP TERMS: Male Ego

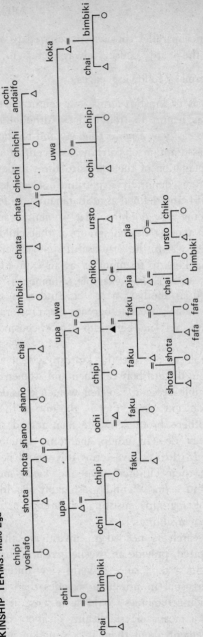

KINSHIP TERMS: Female Ego

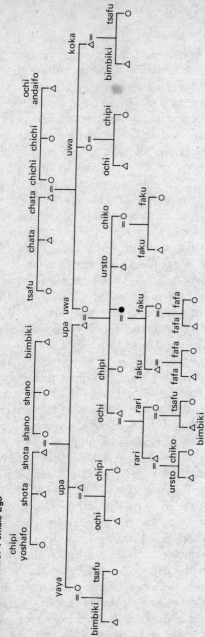
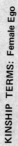

Initiation would be necessary to validate a child's or young adult's inclusion in one and only one descent group.

A moiety interpretation seems partially accurate for the Sharanahua since the closely related Cashinahua have almost precisely the same kinship system and do have named moieties. The Cashinahua are more numerous than the Sharanahua, perhaps slightly less acculturated, and far less prone to exploit affinal ties and use affinal terminology. In terms of the speculation above, the Cashinahua also have initiation ceremonies, the Sharanahua, never. (Kensinger, Kenneth, *Matrilocality and Patrilineality in Cashinahua Society,* (master's essay, University of Pennsylvania, 1964).

The flexibility of Panoan kinship seems to allow for moieties and group endogmy whenever a group is sufficiently numerous, increased importance of affines and marriages to foreigners when the group is small. Gertrude Dole's work among the Amahuaca provides a careful analysis of "The influences of population density on the development of social organization among the Amahuaca of eastern Peru," unpublished manuscript, n.d.

I have several conflicting definitions of *unwu yura* (my kin): one informant tended to identify only agnates, whereas others included bilateral kinsmen as well. To a certain extent this variation was consistent. Baiyakondi's sons, Iconahua and Ndaishiwaka, tended to emphasize the patrilineal line. Both men have successfully avoided uxorilocality and have remained in the same village as their father and brother throughout all the moves of villages. (Despite this, they seldom feel obligated to share food with their father's household, nor do they usually eat with their father.)

In contrast, Basta's and Zacharais' households tend to include bilateral kinsmen as *unwu yura*. When Basta wept over Chicolopez, as described in the text (p. 44), and referred to him as *unwu yura,* the relationship was father's sister's son, *chai.* Yawandi, Basta's daughter, also included Chicolopez as *unwu yura.*

A further puzzle in analyzing Sharanahua kinship is the disparity between the terms *achi* and *koka. Achi* is the only term in the system that is nonreciprocal since it is used only between members of the opposite sex (yet unlike *bimbiki* and *poi* it only applies to females), and women call father's sisters *yaya.* In contrast, *koka* is used both by men and women: *koka-uwa* and *koka-koka.* There seems to be a faint preference for patrilateral cross-cousin marriage, which would make *achi* more often a mother-in-law than *koka* is a father-in-law. The tendency towards uxorilocal residence makes the son in-law–mother-in-law relationship frequent, the daughter-in-law–father-in-law, rare, in terms of actual interactions. The father-daughter relationship, also *upa-achi* is, as discussed in the text, far more important structurally than mother-son, *uwa-koka*.

4. The terms *chiko* and *chipi* seem to have been derived from an old term *chipoku,* which I have only heard a few times in myths. In context it appeared to mean "younger sibling of the same sex," but it was not clear whether it could be used for brothers as well as sisters. It was also translated once as "co-wife," which is consistent with the possible relationship between sisters. In another myth the term *chiku* was used in addressing, "wife."

5. Raiding appears to have been frequent in the past and gaining women in this manner would have allowed young men far more opportunity to take wives yet retain their kinsmen. Given the strong preference for village endogamy, residence would have been at least as often virilocal as uxorilocal in the past.

6. I found two cases of marriages to a first cross-cousin. Several informants said that it is better to marry a distant cross-cousin instead of actual father's sister's daughter or mother's brother's daughter, but there was a good deal of disagreement among informants on this question.

Chapter Four

1. While at any given moment fewer marriages are polygynous than monogamous, men expect eventually to have two wives and, in the past, have expected to have more. Out of 17 marriages, excluding here marriage to children, four are polygynous, and three men were polygynous until their first wife died.

2. Although there is a term *fafama* for women, which is roughly equivalent to *raisi* for men, it is almost never used, and informants were hesitant and varied in their analysis of its application.

3. A record was kept for a 28 day period of the intake and distribution of meat for three households: Baiyakondi's (which at that time included Iconahua and his two wives and children who main-

tained a separate cookhouse and distributed separately and shortly thereafter, moved into their own house) Zacharais', and Basta's.

Game kept in house [1]	Game distributed
Iconahua's	
2 turtles	1 turtle
tapir meat [2]	¼ collared peccary
small bird	
large snail	
spider monkey	
small alligator	
¼ collared peccary [3]	
Baiyakondi's	
howler monkey	¾ collared peccary
small monkey	
tapir meat [2]	
turtle	
¼ collared peccary	
Zacharais'	
small paca	2½ collared peccaries minus 1 head
2 turtles	and 1 back
3 small birds	¼ capybara
½ white-lipped peccary [3]	
¼ capybara [3]	
½ deer [3]	
1 collared peccary plus 1 head and 1 back	
Basta's	
4 turtles	1½ collared peccaries
3 small birds	3 turtles
1 spider monkey	
1 howler monkey	
1 armadillo	
½ collared peccary	

[1] This list does not indicate the quantity of food actually eaten by each household, since it does not include the game that they receive in distribution from other households.

[2] Since a tapir cannot be carried by one man, everyone who went to carry a part, kept that part.

[3] Game has already been shared with a hunting partner before being brought to the house.

Chapter Five

1. For a thorough description of hunting among a closely related people, see Carneiro, Robert, "Hunting and hunting magic among the Amahuaca," *Ethnology* 9:331–41, 1970. I believe his description to apply equally to the Sharanahua, except for their recent preference for shotguns. Also, the Amahuaca bow is longer, averaging between six and six and one-half feet.

2. Hunting and fishing record of four weeks for three sample households: Baiyakondi's, Zacharais', and Basta's.

Household	Hunter	Hunted	Success-ful	Fished	Success-ful [1]
Baiyakondi's	Baiyakondi	0	0	0	0
	Iconahua	5	4	2	2
	Buraya	1	1	4	1
	Sharafo	3	3	2	2
Zacharais'	Zacharais	4	2	2	2
	Samuel	2	0	3	1
	Tohukai	11	4	3	3
	Tararai	3	3	1	1
Basta's	Basta	11	7	4	4
	Gustavo	4	2	4	3

Hunting efforts per household:

	Hunted	Successful
Baiyakondi's	9	8
Zacharais'	20	9
Basta's	15	9

The hunting, fishing, and distribution records (see Chapter Four notes) were kept during April 1966. This is toward the end of the rainy season, a fair period for hunting. These 10 men represented half of the males at Marcos above the age of 16 in 1966. Additional discussion of these figures can be found in Siskind, Janet, *Reluctant Hunters*, doctoral dissertation, Columbia University, 1968.

---

[1] All unsuccessful fishing was lake fishing with bows and arrows.

3. *Fakupa* and *fakuwa* are at times translated as "other husband" and "other wife." These are terms of reference. One either uses the person's name or calls them *bimbiki*. These terms may apply to alternate generations, though I have never heard them so used. Informants, when questioned, stated that they may be used by a man referring to his son's son's wife (*fakuwa*) or a woman to her daughter's daughter's husband (*fakupa*).

4. I have discussed a possible ecological basis for the competition over women and the "meat for sex" syndrome in Siskind, Janet, "Tropical forest hunters and the economy of sex," in Gross, Daniel, ed., *Peoples and Cultures of Native South America*, New York: Doubleday, 1973.

5. The discussion of the role of sex antagonism in supporting and defining male and female groupings derives from Murphy, Robert, "Social structure and sex antagonism," *Southwestern Journal of Anthropology* 15:89–98, 1959.

Chapter Six

1. Although I know of no hunting magic, taboo, or rituals, it is certainly possible that they exist, though following the logic of my analysis I doubt very much that they would be sexual taboos. It is probable that most hunting beliefs would not be shared with a woman. Basta did tell me of herbal medicines, applied externally, which prevent bad luck in hunting, and showed me the plants. Robert Carneiro reports far more extensive hunting ritual for the Amahuaca. No sexual taboos exist, and I suspect that the Sharanahua practices are or were similar, Carneiro, Robert, "Hunting and hunting magic."

2. The manioc beer (*puti*) that the Sharanahua have always made is only slightly fermented to effect the taste. It is nonalcholic. They have learned from Peruvians to ferment it several days and to add cane juice to make the relatively powerful drink called *masato* in Spanish, *bitishu* in Sharanahua. In one myth Yawandi mentioned a fermented beer made from corn, which she said she had heard of in the past. No one else ever mentioned this, however, so I am not sure that this was an accurate memory.

Chapter Seven

1. A collection and analysis of botanical specimens of *ayahuasca,
chacruna,* and the cactus, *chai,* was carried out by Laurent Rivier
at Marcos during the summer of 1969. His findings appear in Rivier,
Laurent, and Lindgren, Jan-Erik, " 'Ayahuasca', the South American
hallucinogenic drink," *Economic Botany* 26:101–29, 1972. See also,
Pinkley, Homer, "Plant admixtures to *ayahuasca,* the South American
hallucinogenic drink," *Lloydia* 32:305–14, 1969.

2. The physiological effects of *ayahuasca* are based on my obversa-
tions and experiences and those of others. In particular, Laurent
Rivier, Isabel Rüf, Oscar Rios, Marlene Dobkin de Rios, and Michael
Harner. Rivier suggested the possible abortive effect of the drug as a
reason for women's usual abstinence. Oscar Rios is pursuing research
on the psycho-physiological effects of the drug and suggests that it
affects the lateral afferent pathways of the reticular formation of the
brain, thus creating a kind of sensory chaos, which would be particularly susceptible to cultural structuring into a learned order.

For further discussions of the effects and cultural uses of *aya-
huasca* see: Harner, Michael, ed., *Hallucinogens and Shamanism,*
New York: Oxford University Press, 1973; Reichel-Dolmatoff,
Gerardo, "The cultural context of an aboriginal hallucinogen;
Banisteriopsis caapi," in Furst, Peter, ed., *Flesh of the Gods,* New
York: Praeger Publishers, 1972, pp. 84–113.

3. The approach to ritual as an attempt at "transformation,"
derives from Wallace, Anthony, *Religion,* New York: Random
House, 1966. The causal and functional discussion is influenced by
Spiro, Melford, "Culture and personality; the natural history of a
false dichotomy," *Psychiatry* 14:19–46, 1951; and Spiro, Melford,
"Problems of definitions and explanations," in Banton, Michael,
ed., *Anthropological Approaches to Religion,* London: Tavistock
Publications Limited, 1966, pp. 85–126.

Chapter Eight

1. I have been struck in considering this scene with Basta and
Gustavo at my own acceptance of the totally contradictory medical
ethic of our culture. I have often asked students if they would

have continued giving medicines to *yura futsa* after this confrontation, and they invariably share my pure thought that one cannot refuse medicines to the sick. Since they know as well as I do that medical care in this culture depends upon the ability to pay, it is a fascinating demonstration of the power of "ideal" over "real" cultural norms. Realistically, Basta and Gustavo were right in trying to limit the number of sick people who came into Marcos since potentially this could rapidly spread illness throughout their village.

2. Among their other herbal medicines, Sharanahua include an abortifacient, which is said to permanently eliminate menstruation and conception. I know one woman who is still within her reproductive years, who has born two children but no more, and says that she took this medicine to prevent further pregnancies. Another woman took the medicine and, nonetheless, became pregnant. When I questioned the efficacy of the medicine I was told that she had not maintained the diet and celibacy that is required for one month after taking the medicine. I remain somewhat skeptical, but Kenneth Kensinger, who spent 11 years with the Cashinahua, is convinced that their medicine is effective.

The usual method of abortion appears to be completely successful. This is by direct pressure on the uterus, during or before the third month of pregnancy. Sharanahua women practice abortion in order to space children at approximately three-year intervals. This is the nursing period, and they feel it is too difficult for a woman to nurse two children and dangerous to wean below the age of three. It is believed that when twins are born, one will not survive. Only two cases of twins were described, both some time in the past. They are said to have died by sorcery. Abortion is also practiced if a woman decides she has had enough children and wishes to avoid the pains of childbirth, or, as mentioned above, if a girl is considered too young to bear a child.

3. An earlier version of parts of this chapter appears under the title of "Visions and cures among the Sharanahua," in Harner, ed., *Hallucinogens and Shamanism.*

4. I found three sources extremely helpful in this analysis of the shaman-patient communication: Lévi-Strauss, Claude, "The

sorcerer and his magic," and "The effectiveness of symbols," in *Structural Anthropology*, Jacobsen, Claire and Schoepf, Brooke, trans., New York: Basic Books, 1963; and Geertz, Clifford, "Religion as a cultural system," in Banton, ed., *Anthropological Approaches to Religion*, pp. 1–46.

5.   In a general survey of psychotherapy, Jerome Frank makes the point that any medical practice that is not actually harmful will relieve symptoms a good deal of the time: Frank, Jerome, *Persuasion and Healing*, New York: Schocken Books, 1963. This statement makes it possible to avoid a fruitless discussion of whether singing and hallucinating are a more or less effective curing method than a belief in the Virgin of Lourdes or in little white pills.

6.   Two women, Yawanini and Yawandi, are particularly skilled in assisting at births and are called for difficult cases. It may be only coincidental that their names are similar and that the first syllable of both, "Ya," is also the first syllable of Yapi, the Mouse-Spirit, who teaches women how to give birth. I never questioned this since I did not notice it in the field. Although the two names are spelled differently in the text to avoid confusion, phonetically they should both be spelled Yawandi and Yawandidi.

  I have never seen a birth at Marcos, although one infant was born while I was in the village. I had been told that women go alone or with another woman to help them into the forest nearby to give birth. However, the birth that occurred while I was there took place in the woman's house.

7.   Students have often commented on or questioned possible similarities between the shaman and a psychoanalyst. In my view the shaman is more priest than psychoanalyst. The communication between shaman and patient at Marcos resembles in part the communication of dream symbols between analyst and patient in our culture, but the message communicated by the shaman is usually an "adjustment" or conservative message. This is not generally a productive message in psychoanalysis. See Pearce, Jane, and Newton, Saul, *The Conditions of Human Growth*, New York: The Citadel Press, 1963.

Chapter Nine

1. The prices in *soles* and their dollar equivalents are based on the exchange rate of 1967, which was 27 *soles* to 1 dollar.

2. The story of the competition over money between Echigeray and Gamboa was told to me by Isabel Rüf. Miss Rüf, who worked with the Culina at Zapote, also told me the Culina version of the death of Alberto. The Culina claimed that when they threw *dori* death took only a few hours, and the fact that Alberto took three days to die established their innocence. The Sharanahua were not convinced.

INDEX